NICOLA GRAIMES

# NEW VEGETARIAN KITCHEN

raw / broil / fry / steam / simmer / bake

DUNCAN BAIRD PUBLISHERS

LONDON

For Silvio, Ella and Jool, with love.

# NEW VEGETARIAN KITCHEN
Nicola Graimes

Distributed in the USA and Canada by
Sterling Publishing Co., Inc.
387 Park Avenue South
New York, NY 10016-8810

First published in the UK and USA in 2011 by
Duncan Baird Publishers Ltd
Sixth Floor, Castle House
75–76 Wells Street
London W1T 3QH

Copyright © Duncan Baird Publishers 2011
Text copyright © Nicola Graimes 2011
Photography copyright © Duncan Baird Publishers 2011

The right of Nicola Graimes to be identified as the Author of
this text has been asserted in accordance with the Copyright,
Designs and Patents Act of 1988.

All rights reserved. No part of this book may be reproduced in
any form or by any electronic or mechanical means, including
information storage and retrieval systems, without permission
in writing from the publisher, except by a reviewer who may
quote brief passages in a review.

Managing Editor: Grace Cheetham
Editor: Nicole Bator
Designer: Luana Gobbo
Commissioned photography: William Lingwood
Photography Assistant: Isobel Wield
Food Stylist: Bridget Sargeson
Food Stylist Assistants: Jack Sargeson and Katy McClelland
Prop Stylist: Wei Tang

Library of Congress Cataloging-in-Publication Data available

ISBN: 978-1-84483-926-1

10 9 8 7 6 5 4 3 2 1

Typeset in Conduit, Bodoni and Filosofia
Color reproduction by Colourscan
Printed in China by Imago

For information about custom editions, special sales, premium
and corporate purchases, please contact Sterling Special Sales
Department at 800-805-5489 or specialsales@sterlingpub.com.

**Publisher's note:** While every care has been taken in compiling
the recipes for this book, Duncan Baird Publishers, or any other
persons who have been involved in working on this publication,
cannot accept responsibility for any errors or omissions,
inadvertent or not, that may be found in the recipes or text, nor
for any problems that may arise as a result of preparing one
of these recipes. If you are pregnant or breastfeeding or have
any special dietary requirements or medical conditions, it is
advisable to consult a medical professional before following any
of the recipes contained in this book.

### What is a vegetarian?

A vegetarian is someone who does not eat meat, poultry,
seafood, or other animal-derived by-products, such as gelatin.

### Notes on the recipes

• Cheese, especially those made using traditional methods, may
contain calf rennet, so check labels first. Look for 'suitable for
vegetarians', the 'V' sign or 'contains vegetarian rennet' on the
label. All cheeses used in the following recipes are available in a
vegetarian form.

### Unless otherwise stated:

• Use large eggs and medium fruit and vegetables
• Use ripe fruit and fresh herbs
• Use unsalted butter
• 1 tsp = 5ml • 1 tbsp = 15ml • 1 cup = 240ml

### Acknowledgements

My sincere thanks go to Grace Cheetham for commissioning me
to write this book and for her continued enthusiasm and having
faith in me. Thank you also to my fantastic editor, Nicole Bator,
who was a huge inspiration and generously shared her talent,
and kept me going with her positive feedback. I would also like
to express my huge gratitude to the rest of the team behind the
book, designer Luana Gobbo, William Lingwood for the great
photography, food stylist Bridget Sargeson and props stylist
Wei Tang.

# CONTENTS

# INTRODUCTION

This book has been a long time in the making. What began as a little seed of an idea many years ago has evolved and developed into a collection of recipes I couldn't be more excited about sharing. Gone are the old standbys long associated with vegetarian food. In their place are fresh, modern recipes that broaden the appeal of meat-free cuisine, giving vegetarians lots of new ideas and tempting even the most adamant meat-eater with adventurous, irresistible flavors.

I came to food writing in a back-to-front sort of way, from my time as a food editor with a love of cooking to being given the wonderful opportunity to write my own book many years ago. But vegetarian cooking has always been a passion, and I love the challenge of planning and developing a dish. For me, vegetables are too often considered an afterthought, plonked on the side of the plate, playing second fiddle to the other foods they're served with. And too often a vegetarian "meal" is unbalanced, with lots of carbohydrate but little or no protein. That's why this book focuses primarily on recipes that are "complete" meals in themselves, with both a protein and carbohydrate, rather than a collection of insubstantial side dishes.

Truth be told, I didn't really want this book to be classified as a "vegetarian" book. Instead, it's more a celebration of the ingredients I love, from fresh produce, herbs, spices, and legumes to grains, nuts, cheese, eggs, and more. It's the quality, nuances, and versatility of these foods that I wanted to highlight, and the fact that the recipes happen to exclude meat, poultry, fish, and seafood is really just incidental.

I'm actually quite an impatient cook and most the of time I just want to create something delicious and, usually, nutritious, as easily and quickly as possible. Many of the recipes in this book satisfy these criteria, but they're balanced with others that take a little more time and effort. Either way, the principal aim is to get the best out of ingredients by exploring different ways of preparing and cooking them. Presentation is also key. This doesn't mean spending lots of time fiddling with food on the plate but, more importantly, thinking visually and considering how ingredients work together in terms of color, texture, flavor, and temperature. It can be as simple as sprinkling some fresh herbs or crushed, toasted nuts over a dish to add color or crunch.

The cuisines of the world are a huge inspiration to me, so you'll find recipes influenced by dishes from as far afield as Japan and Indonesia to Italy and the Caribbean—all with a contemporary, and sometimes a fusion, twist. I created all of the recipes for the home kitchen, and even the most novice cook is guaranteed to succeed with them. If you're already very confident in the kitchen, these recipes will provide you with a fresh approach and plenty of new ideas to start trying.

## ABOUT THIS BOOK

Understanding the basics about cooking techniques gives you great freedom to experiment, be creative, and bring out the best in the ingredients you use. Choosing to broil, steam, or fry an ingredient, for example, will alter its taste, texture, and appearance. Take an onion: slow-cooking curbs its pungency and gives it a meltingly soft texture, while stir-frying results in a slightly crunchy and more intensely flavored taste, and a raw onion is crisp and sharp.

*New Vegetarian Kitchen* highlights the six core techniques you'll use to make outstanding meals: raw, broil, fry, steam, simmer, and bake. Each one has its own benefits and idiosyncrasies. Most ingredients are better suited to certain cooking techniques than to others, so the basics of each technique are explained in the following pages and the recipes show you which ones to use when. Of course, many recipes are a combination of different techniques that work in harmony to create a finished dish. When more than one method is used in a recipe, the recipe is found under the primary technique.

This is not a handbook to cooking techniques but rather a showcase of the possibilities that each technique presents. It's about being adventurous and playing around with flavors, colors, and textures to make sensational meat-free meals. I've also included guidance on how to cook certain ingredients, such as rice and dried legumes, and there's a handy glossary you can refer to if you're baffled by any of the more unusual ingredients featured in the recipes.

## RAW

Bright and vibrant in color, crisp and crunchy in texture, and quite different in taste to cooked dishes, meals created with uncooked ingredients can be surprisingly diverse and inspiring. By experimenting with marinating, grinding, blending, chopping, slicing, and freezing foods, you can create a stunning array of dishes that are colorful, fresh, and nutritious. This chapter focuses on getting the best out of uncooked ingredients, whether it be a garlicky Chilled Almond Soup or a Savory Cheesecake with Red Pepper and Cilantro Relish.

It's common sense, but so often forgotten, that variations in texture and consistency influence taste and also affect the way an ingredient integrates with others on a plate. For example, preparing a raw carrot in myriad ways can produce varying end results: a thickly sliced carrot tastes quite different from one that is coarsely grated, pureed, or juiced.

Being adventurous with presentation contributes to a dish's overall success, too. Preparing fresh fruit and vegetables, nuts, seeds, herbs, and spices in different ways enhances their visual impact on the plate.

Many of the dishes in this chapter adhere to the principles of the raw food diet (broadly defined as foods that are uncooked or warmed to a temperature no greater than 104°F). Others feature a main ingredient that is uncooked but can be combined with cooked foods, such as cheese, or canned beans to add extra substance and complement the raw ingredients. Even though there's no full-on cooking in these recipes, they will offer you new ways of combining raw ingredients to make delicious meals.

## BROIL

Broiling relies on applying intense, dry heat from above to the surface of a food and is used to quickly brown or caramelize. It lends a dish a slightly smoky, toasted, or barbecued flavor, depending on what you are cooking. In fact, the broiler can be used as an alternative to the barbecue.

Successful broiling is influenced by two things: temperature and the distance the food is placed from the heat source. The dry, intense heat of a broiler is perfect for a number of things. You can brown the top of a gratin or pie or finish cooking dishes, such as a frittata or Spanish tortilla. Broiling is also great for melting cheese and giving a golden glaze to marinated vegetables, fruit, and tofu. Broiling also provides a healthier, low-fat alternative to frying foods such as burgers and fritters.

Certain cheeses, particularly halloumi, mozzarella, goat cheese crottin, and feta, are especially suited to broiling, since they melt, soften, or brown but still retain their shape. Eggplants, peppers, zucchini, mushrooms, and tomatoes are just a few of my favorite vegetables for broiling. I slice them fairly thinly, brush with oil, and broil until softened and charred in places. Grilling vegetables this way is often much faster than it would normally take to roast them, and the flavor is fabulous.

Apples, pears, peaches, pineapple, mango, bananas, and many other fruits—perhaps with the exclusion of berries—are suitable for broiling as well, since the dry heat helps to caramelize the sugars found naturally in the fruit. Heat the broiler until very hot, then sprinkle the fruit with sugar or drizzle with honey and arrange it in a single layer on baking parchment paper. Position the baking sheet about 3 inches from the heat and broil until softened and golden—deliciously simple.

## FRY

There are many variations of frying, each dependent upon the quantity of oil, the level of heat, the type of pan used and the amount the food is stirred or tossed in the pan during cooking.

Sautéing is great for cooking small, evenly sized pieces of food quickly in a little oil or butter, tossing them regularly until browned. A wide, shallow pan with straight sides and a heavy base is perfect for this technique. The fat should be preheated in the pan over medium-high heat until "shimmering" but not smoking (butter will become foamy.) If the fat is too cool, then whatever you are sautéing will not brown and may absorb the fat, becoming greasy. You want just enough oil to coat the bottom of the pan and when hot, add your ingredients and toss until beginning to crisp—if they start to burn you may wish to reduce the heat slightly. For the best flavor, try using a combination of oil and butter but depending on the style of cooking, adapt the type of fat you use, using olive oil in Mediterranean dishes, for instance.

Pan-frying uses slightly less heat (medium to medium-low) than sautéing and only a small to moderate amount of fat. It's more suitable for larger pieces of food that don't require tossing or constant stirring but are simply turned over occasionally.

Griddling differs from other methods of frying in that the food, rather than the pan, is oiled, which ensures the characteristic seared or charred marks and the wonderful slightly smoky flavor of griddled foods. When buying a griddle pan, make sure it's made from heavy cast iron so it can be heated to a very high temperature without buckling. It should be heated before adding food so the heat sears the outside almost straightaway but retains moisture inside. Vegetables take on a new dimension when griddled, as do tofu, tempeh, and halloumi, which hold their shape during cooking. Thick slices of griddled bread, such as ciabatta or baguette, drizzled with oil, rubbed with garlic, and topped with tomato make the perfect bruschetta.

Shallow-frying is used for browning the outside of foods such as vegetable fritters or burgers, while sealing in moisture and flavor. It uses more oil than sautéing, pan-frying or stir-frying—the food being cooked is half-submerged in hot oil and is normally turned over halfway through cooking. It's a good idea to cook the "presentation" side first for the best appearance. A heavy-bottomed skillet is best for shallow-frying, because it ensures even heat distribution.

Deep-fried foods should have a crisp, golden exterior, and tender middle—they should never be greasy or soggy. Deep-frying is ideal for cooking foods such as doughnuts, fritters, gyoza, and potatoes, and for things coated in batter or bread crumbs. It's a quick method of cooking and the food should be completely submerged in the hot oil. The right type of oil is crucial: sunflower, peanut, and canola oils are ideal because of their mild flavor and high smoking point, which means they remain stable when heated to a high temperature. The temperature of the oil is also important to make sure the middle of the food is cooked and the exterior crisp but not burned. Use a kitchen thermometer to monitor the temperature as you heat the oil, or try the bread test: heat the oil until it gives off a smoky haze, then drop in a cube of day-old bread and time how long it takes to brown. The list below explains the approximate time it takes to brown the bread at the given temperature.

- Low heat: 60 seconds = 315°F
- Medium heat: 40 seconds = 350°F
- High heat: 20 seconds = 375°F

Choose a pan that has deep sides but isn't too large and cumbersome. Importantly, do not fill it more than two-thirds full with oil. If using a basket, dip it in the hot oil before adding the food to prevent the food from sticking to it. After cooking, remove the food from the oil with a slotted spoon and drain well on paper towels. Deep-fried food is best served immediately, but if you need to keep it warm before serving, avoid covering the food or it will become soggy. Instead, put it in a single layer on a plate or baking sheet and keep it in a warm oven with the door ajar to let air circulate.

Stir-frying is an excellent, quick method of cooking food. It preserves valuable nutrients and retains the food's flavor, color, and texture. If you expect to do a lot of stir-frying, it's worth investing in a good wok, which is usually fairly inexpensive. The best modern woks are made from lightweight carbon steel, which is a good heat conductor and becomes nonstick when "seasoned" properly and looked after. You can also deep-fry, steam, and braise in a wok, so choose a size that suits a wide range of cooking methods and is not too small. A wok that measures 12 to 14 inches across the top is a good size to aim for.

Preparation is key when stir-frying: make sure the vegetables are cut into uniform-size pieces so they cook evenly, and measure all liquid ingredients before you begin. Certain oils are better than others, so choose one with a mild flavor and high smoking point, such as those recommended for deep-frying. The first step to successful stir-frying is to heat the wok over high heat before you add the oil, then add the foods that take the longest to cook, such as onions, carrots, and so on, leaving other ingredients like leafy greens, bean sprouts, and flavorings to ensure everything cooks evenly and reaches the right temperature. If you don't have a wok, a large, heavy-bottomed skillet is also suitable for stir-frying.

## STEAM

Steaming allows foods to retain their texture, shape, and flavor and can revive dried ingredients by adding moisture. An important technique in Asian cooking, steaming is highly regarded for its relative ease and restorative qualities. Because foods are cooked in moist heat, rather than in fat or oil, steaming is one of the healthiest cooking techniques you can choose, and it's particularly good for delicate foods, vegetables, fruits, puddings, dumplings, grains and foods steamed in packages.

There are two methods of steaming: direct and indirect. Direct steaming is the most common and involves placing a perforated basket over bubbling water and then covering with a lid. The food cooks in the rising steam without coming into direct contact with the liquid. The steam must be able to circulate freely during cooking, so avoid overfilling the steamer basket or the food close to the lid will discolor and become soggy as the condensation that forms on the lid drips onto it. Half-full is ideal. Tiered bamboo steamers, found in Asian food stores, are especially designed for this purpose and can be placed over a wok of simmering water. Vegetables and dumplings are usually cooked this way.

The indirect method of steaming is used for cooking steamed sweet and savory puddings, as well as rice. The sealed pudding bowl is placed on a trivet or upturned saucer in a large pan, then boiling water is poured in until it comes halfway up the sides of the bowl. This method of steaming tends to be very slow, because it takes a while for the heat to reach the middle of the pudding, but it does give a light, open texture to a pudding. Two points to remember when steaming a pudding: avoid lifting the lid off the pan during the first 30 minutes because the drop in temperature can make the pudding sink. Also, keep an eye on water levels and occasionally top up with more boiling water, if necessary.

## SIMMER

Simmering is the technique used to cook food in gently bubbling liquid, be it water, stock, wine, or juice. It lets the flavors of the ingredients merge and enhance each other, while still retaining their individual character.

Poaching is a perfect method for cooking foods, such as certain fruits, vegetables, and eggs. Poaching is normally done at a lower temperature than simmering: Submerge the food in liquid and cook over low heat so the liquid barely trembles. It's great for slightly underripe fruit — in fact, avoid using very ripe fruit, because it will disintegrate during cooking. Vegetables such as fennel, carrots, potatoes, and zucchini also poach well in stock and make a light, flavorful stew or soup.

Poaching softens and sweetens fruit and is well suited to cherries, pears, peaches, nectarines, and apricots. Submerge the fruit in a sugar syrup, wine, or fruit juice, which can be flavored with spices, such as cinnamon, ginger, cardamom, or vanilla. If the fruit is likely to discolor, add a splash of lemon juice to prevent this.

To poach an egg, first crack it into a cup, then lower it into a sauté pan or small saucepan filled with about 2 inches barely simmering water. (Some recommend swirling the water first to make a whirlpool, which encourages the egg to form a neat circle.) Raise the heat slightly so the water is gently bubbling and cook 2 to 3 minutes until the white is set but the yolk remains runny. Remove the egg from the water with a slotted spoon and let it drain slightly, then serve warm.

Stewing is similar to poaching but uses less liquid. It's suitable for most fruit, transforming them into a thick sauce or compote. The fruit can then be passed through a strainer to make a puree or coulis. Stewing is also the ideal method for cooking hearty winter fare, such as savory stews, casseroles, and soups. Some curries also benefit from stewing over a low, gentle heat, increasing the heat of the chili and helping to meld the complex individual flavors of the spices. The beauty of this cooking technique is that dishes can be fully (or partially) cooked ahead of time and then reheated—remarkably often tasting better with time since the flavors are slowly and gently coaxed out.

Both poaching and stewing are particularly useful if you a have a glut of fruit you want to preserve, either as whole fruit, a thick compote, or jam for future use.

Braising involves slow-cooking a food that is half-submerged in liquid. The pan is covered and the food is cooked for a longer period than boiling or simmering.  The cooking liquid is mostly absorbed into the food, producing a tender result, and there is usually some liquid left in the pan, which can be used as a sauce.

Finally, boiling is vigorous and fast, with the heat set at a high temperature. When cooking pasta or noodles, it's important to keep them at a rolling boil to prevent the strands sticking together. Similarly, dense vegetables, such as potatoes and other root vegetables, often require boiling to soften them. Eggs, on the other hand, should not be boiled hard, but simmered in gently bubbling water, as vigorous boiling can crack the shells, toughen the whites, and discolor the egg yolks.

Some of the recipes call for a vegetable to be blanched. This involves partially cooking it by boiling, then refreshing it under cold running water to stop the cooking process. It can then be cooked to completion just before serving.

## BAKE

There is nothing more appealing than the intoxicating aroma of freshly baked bread. More than any other cooking technique, baking tells you when a food is ready by filling the kitchen with wonderful aromas.

The terms "bake" and "roast" are often used interchangeably, and there's really no hard and fast rule that distinguishes them. In both cases, food is cooked in the dry heat of an oven at temperatures usually above 300°F. Rather loosely, "baking" tends to be used for breads, cakes, cookies, pastries, and pies. But then there are baked potatoes, fruit, stews, gratins, and pasta dishes. "Roasting" usually involves the use of fat to encourage a crisp or golden exterior and moist interior; it usually refers to savory foods – although, again, there are many exceptions to this generalization.

Successful baking demands certain practices. Firstly, the oven needs to be preheated. This allows the food to start cooking at the correct temperature as soon as it's put in the oven, which is key. If you have a fan convection oven, check the manufacturer's recommendations for how to adjust baking times accordingly. Next, make sure you use the right size pan or baking dish, otherwise the cooking time and texture of the food can be affected. For some dishes, such as casseroles and gratins, this might not be crucial, but cakes and other baked foods certainly require accuracy. It's worth investing in good-quality, heavy-duty trays and pans, too. They last longer, conduct heat evenly, and do not warp at high temperatures.

Fruit is great for baking. The heat of the oven softens the cells of the fruit and intensifies its flavor by drying it slightly. Fruit can also be dry roasted to preserve it, as well as to intensify its sweetness. This requires a low temperature and can take some time to extract the moisture from the fruit. Tomatoes also work well cooked in this way, and it's a great method for preserving a summer glut.

It's important when baking/roasting fruit and vegetables that they fit comfortably in an even layer in the pan, without overcrowding, to guarantee they become golden and slightly caramelized, rather than cooking in their own moisture. Piling them on top of each other will trap in steam and cause them to become soggy instead of golden. If the baking tray is crowded, use two trays instead of one and swap their positions in the oven halfway through cooking. Foods with a high moisture content, such as tomatoes, zucchini and eggplant, will need more space than relatively dry foods, such as potatoes and root vegetables.

Vegetables and fruit can also be baked "en papillote," or in a package, which seals in juices and helps to retain the nuances of any added flavorings.

## LEGUMES, RICE AND SPROUTS

Here are some basic instructions for cooking dried legumes and rice, and for sprouting your own legumes or seeds.

### LEGUMES

Legumes make an invaluable contribution to a meat-free diet and are versatile and nutritious. The recipes in this book call for "cooked" beans, which can either be cooked from scratch or canned. The former need a little advanced preparation but are more economical and taste better. There is much debate as to whether soaking dried beans before cooking is necessary. Lentils do not need soaking, but soaking certainly reduces the cooking time for other beans, including split peas, and can enhance their flavor because it starts the germination process.

Begin with rinsing the dried beans, then soak them in cold water for a minimum of 4 hours or overnight if more convenient (soaking them for more than 4 hours has little influence on the cooking time). Drain and rinse the beans again, then put them in a saucepan and cover with 1 inch cold water. Bring to a boil and boil rapidly 10 minutes, then reduce the heat and simmer the beans, partially covered, until tender, 45 minutes to 1 hour 30 minutes, depending on the bean.

If you are short of time, the long soaking process can be speeded up: first cook the dried beans in boiling water 2 minutes, then remove the pan from the heat, cover, and let stand about 2 hours. Drain, rinse, and cover with fresh cold water before cooking, as described above.

Avoid adding salt or any acidic ingredients to the beans during cooking as this prevents them from softening. Some cooks add baking soda to the water to help soften the legumes, but this can reduce their nutritional value.

Dried legumes roughly double in weight and volume when cooked, so bear this in mind when following the recipes. All of the recipes call for "cooked" beans, so if you are using dried beans, reduce the quantity called for by half and prepare as above. A drained 15-ounce can is roughly the equivalent of ¾ cup dried beans. If using canned beans, rinse and drain them before use.

## RICE

There are many methods of cooking rice, depending on preference and type, but the classic method for cooking boiled rice with fluffy, separate grains is the absorption method. Use a long-grain white rice, such as basmati, and rinse the rice in several changes of water until it runs clear. Put the rice in a heavy-bottomed saucepan and cover with about 1½ times the quantity of water or stock (it should be covered by about ½ inch of fluid). Bring to a boil, uncovered, then turn the heat down to its lowest setting, cover with a lid, and simmer about 10 minutes, or until the water is absorbed. Remove the pan from the heat and let stand, covered, 10 minutes, then fluff up the grains of rice with a fork to separate the grains.

## SPROUTING LEGUMES AND SEEDS

Sprouted beans are incredibly nutritious and add flavor and crunch to a dish. To grow your own, soak a handful of dried legumes or seeds, such as mung beans, lentils, or alfalfa, in lukewarm water overnight. Drain well, then transfer to a clean, sterilized jar. Cover the jar with a small piece of cheesecloth, secure with a rubber band, and let stand in a warm, light place. Rinse, in the jar, twice a day under cold running water, draining well each time. The sprouts will be ready in 3 to 5 days. Transfer to an airtight container and store up to five days in the refrigerator.

## INGREDIENTS

Some recipes in this book use ingredients that you might be unfamiliar with or have heard of but not used. Here is a brief list of some of the more unusual:

BARBERRIES—These small, dark red dried berries have a sharp, sour flavor and are popular in Middle Eastern cuisine. They're available in Middle Eastern food stores.

CHICKPEA FLOUR—Also known as gram flour or besan, this pale yellow flour is commonly used in Indian cooking. It gives a distinct flavor and texture to foods.

CHINESE BLACK BEANS—These fermented, salted black soybeans are available canned, in packets or dried at good Asian grocery stores. They need to be rinsed before use, and dried beans must be soaked in hot water 20 minutes and rinsed well before use. They become very soft after soaking and can be used whole or ground to a paste as a substitute for bottled black bean sauce.

CHIPOTLE PASTE—A spicy paste made from smoked dried jalapeño peppers that is popular in Mexican cooking. Also look for dried chipotle chilies, which can be used dried in stews or soaked in hot water until softened and ground into a paste.

CURRY LEAVES—These small pointed leaves have a spicy flavor and often feature in Indian cooking. They can be frozen—use straight from the freezer—or dried.

DAIKON—A large, white root vegetable with a radishy flavor. Also known as mooli

ENOKI MUSHROOMS—Native to Japan, these long-stemmed mushrooms grow in clumps and have tiny white caps.

HARISSA—A chili paste made with piri-piri chilies, spices, and tomatoes.

KABOCHA SQUASH—This Japanese winter squash has a dark green skin and vibrant, sweet orange flesh.

KECAP MANIS—This dark, thick, sweet soy sauce used in Indonesian and Malaysian cooking is now widely available, but if you can't find it substitute with dark soy sauce sweetened with a little sugar.

MIRIN—This sweet rice wine is used mainly in Japanese cooking in sauces, marinades, and dressings.

MISO—A paste made from fermented soybeans, varying in color from white and yellow to brown and red; generally, the lighter the color, the milder the flavor.

NORI—Seaweed that is formed into paperlike sheets, then dried. It's used as a wrapping for sushi or sold in flakes for sprinkling over dishes.

POMEGRANATE MOLASSES—A thick, dark, tangy syrup from the Middle East. It can be used in marinades and dressings or mixed with water to make a drink.

PRESERVED LEMONS—Popular in Moroccan cooking, these lemons are preserved in a salty brine, sometimes with added herbs and spices. They can be used in tagines and stews, or finely chopped in salads and dressings.

QUINOA—This protein-rich, gluten-free grain has a mild, slightly bitter flavor

RAMEN NOODLES—These Japanese noodles, made from wheat flour and egg, are often served in a broth of the same name.

RAS-EL-HANOUT—A popular North African blend of herbs and spices that is traditionally used in tagines. Some varieties contain as many as fifty ingredients.

RAW CACAO—Also known as raw chocolate, this is an antioxidant-rich, relatively unprocessed alternative to regular chocolate. Available in nibs and powder form.

RICE PAPER WRAPPERS—Dried, fragile circles of paper-thin rice paper. These need to be soaked briefly in boiled water before use.

SHAOXING WINE—A Chinese fermented rice wine with a slightly sweet taste, reminiscent of dry sherry.

SOBA NOODLES—Made from buckwheat flour or a mixture of wheat and buckwheat, these Japanese noodles are popular served warm or cold.

SUMAC—A sour, slightly astringent, reddish-brown spice that comes from the dried berries of a bush that grows in the Mediterranean and the Middle East.

TAMARIND—A large, brown bean-like pod commonly sold as a paste, a block of compressed pulp (often with seeds), or pureed. It adds a sweet-sour flavor to Asian, Middle Eastern, and Caribbean dishes.

TEMPEH—Made by fermenting soybeans with a cultured starter, rather like cheese-making, tempeh has a nutty, savory flavor and firm texture.

TOGARASHI (SHICHIMI)—A Japanese spice blend made with ground chilies, orange peel, ground sansho, sesame seeds, poppy seeds, hemp seeds, and nori.

TOFU—Made from ground soybeans, tofu is available in various textures, from firm, which holds its shape during cooking, to silken, which is very soft, smooth, and creamy. Abura-age is a deep-fried golden tofu pocket that can be stuffed.

UME PLUM SEASONING—A tart, tangy seasoning made from the juices left over from the pickling of Japanese ume plums.

VEGETARIAN FISH SAUCE—Usually a combination of soybeans, salt, sugar, chili, and citric acid. Found in Thai and Vietnamese food stores.

WAKAME—This curly-leaf, brown seaweed is sold dried. After rehydrating, it has a soft texture and mild vegetable flavor.

WASABI—A pungent condiment made from Japanese horseradish.

Fresh and vibrant, these creative recipes show how easy it is to coax the best out of uncooked ingredients. They rely on techniques such as soaking, marinating, blending, or slicing foods into paper-thin, translucent slivers and elegant "noodles" to create a tantalizing combination of flavors, textures, and colors.

# RAW

Beet Carpaccio with Goat Cheese and Orange–Balsamic Vinaigrette, page 24

# VIETNAMESE RICE PAPER ROLLS WITH PEANUT NUOC CHAM

Nuoc cham is the classic accompaniment to most savory snacks and appetizers in Vietnam. This condiment is traditionally a mix of hot, sweet, sour, and salty flavors and enlivens whatever it is served with, such as these delicious vegetable-filled rice paper rolls.

**SERVES 4 TO 6**

6 scallions, shredded

1 yellow bell pepper, seeded and cut into thin strips

1 carrot, cut into matchsticks

¾ cup finely shredded Chinese leaves

2 tablespoons peeled and finely chopped ginger root

2 garlic cloves, crushed

2 handfuls of bean sprouts

2 tablespoons sweet chili sauce

2 tablespoons light soy sauce

2 teaspoons sesame oil

24 medium rice paper wrappers

4 long chives

4 ounces enoki mushrooms, trimmed and split into 4 or 6 bundles

**NUOC CHAM DIPPING SAUCE**

½ small cucumber, seeded and diced

1 garlic clove, crushed

2 teaspoons palm sugar or light brown sugar

1 bird's-eye chili, finely chopped

2 tablespoons vegetarian fish sauce

juice of 1 lime

2 tablespoons light soy sauce

1 tablespoon roasted peanuts, coarsely chopped

1 Put the scallions, yellow pepper, carrot, Chinese leaves, ginger root, garlic, and bean sprouts in a large mixing bowl. In a small bowl, mix together the chili sauce, soy sauce, and sesame oil. Pour the mixture over the vegetables and toss well.

2 Fill a heatproof bowl with boiled water. Put 2 rice paper wrappers on top of one another (you will need 2 per roll as they are very fragile) and soak in the water 20 seconds, or until they are pliable and opaque. Use a metal spatula to carefully remove the wrappers from the water and drain for a second, then place flat on a plate. Pat dry with paper towel, then spread a spoonful of the vegetable mixture vertically down the middle of the top wrapper. Fold the bottom edge over to enclose the filling and make a bottom, then roll the wrapper over the filling from left to right, leaving the top open. Repeat with the remaining wrappers and filling to make 12 rolls in total.

3 Tie 1 chive around each bundle of enoki mushrooms.

4 Mix together all of the ingredients for the nuoc cham dipping sauce and divide it into four small bowls.

5 Serve 2–3 rice paper rolls per person, accompanied by the dipping sauce and an enoki bundle.

# TRIO OF CASHEW NUT CHEESES

Soaked and blended cashews make a remarkably creamy soft "cheese." Garlic and lemon, herbs, and nuts are just a few of the many flavorings you can use.

**SERVES 4**

2 cups cashew nuts
½ teaspoon salt
1 garlic clove, crushed
1 tablespoon lemon juice
a large pinch of smoked paprika
5 tablespoons shelled pistachios, finely chopped
5 tablespoons chopped mixed herbs, such as thyme, oregano, and chives
freshly ground black pepper
savory crackers, to serve

**1** Put the cashews in a bowl, cover with warm water, and let soak at least 2 hours, then drain and transfer the cashews to a food processor or blender. Add ¾ cup water and blend into a coarse paste. (For a softer "cheese," add a little more water and blend into a coarse puree.) Add the salt and season with pepper.

**2** Divide the nut cheese into 3 equal portions. Stir the garlic, lemon juice, and paprika into 1 portion, then spoon it into a ramekin. Put the chopped pistachios on a plate. Using your hands, divide another portion of the nut cheese into teaspoon-size balls, then roll each ball in the pistachios until evenly coated. Roll the last portion of the nut cheese into a log and roll it in the herbs to coat. Serve the flavored nut cheeses with crackers.

# NECTARINE, BOCCONCINI, AND BASIL SALAD WITH VERJUICE DRESSING

Verjuice is the unfermented juice of unripe wine grapes and makes a refreshing alternative to lemon juice or wine vinegar in salad dressings. If you can't get hold of bocconcini (baby mozzarella cheese), use a single ball of mozzarella sliced into rounds. Serve with crusty bread.

**SERVES 4**

3 tablespoons pine nuts
3 nectarines, halved, pitted, and sliced
10 ounces bocconcini (baby mozzarella), drained
1 handful of basil leaves, roughly torn

VERJUICE DRESSING
3 tablespoons olive oil
1 tablespoon verjuice
salt and freshly ground black pepper

**1** Toast the pine nuts in a dry skillet and over medium heat 3 to 4 minutes, stirring occasionally, until lightly browned. Watch carefully so they do not burn. Remove from the heat and set aside.

**2** In a small bowl, mix together olive oil and verjuice for the dressing and season with salt and pepper.

**3** Arrange the nectarine slices in a shallow dish and top with the bocconcini. Sprinkle with the basil leaves and drizzle with the dressing. Top with the pine nuts and serve.

# BEET CARPACCIO WITH GOAT CHEESE AND ORANGE—BALSAMIC VINAIGRETTE

**SERVES 4**

2 tablespoons orange juice

½ teaspoon balsamic vinegar

¼ cup olive oil

¼ teaspoon salt

1 beet, peeled

½ teaspoon lemon juice

2 large handfuls of mixed leaves, such as watercress and arugula

3½ ounces goat cheese, thinly sliced into rounds

2 tablespoons pumpkin seeds

freshly ground black pepper

1 Put the orange juice, vinegar, oil, and salt in a bowl and beat or blend with an immersion blender until well mixed and thick, then set aside.

2 Using a very sharp knife or a mandolin, cut the beet into paper-thin round slices. Put them in a bowl with the lemon juice and add just enough cold water to cover.

3 Divide the mixed leaves onto four plates, then top with the drained beet and goat cheese, alternating the two in a row across the mixed leaves. Sprinkle with the pumpkin seeds and drizzle with the vinaigrette, then season with black pepper and serve.

# BLACK OLIVE TAPENADE, DOLCELATTE, AND PINE NUT WRAPS

**SERVES 4**

3 tablespoons pine nuts

4 large multiseed tortillas

1 large handful of baby spinach leaves, tough stems removed

1 small red bell pepper, seeded and cut into thin strips

generous ½ cup creamy dolcelatte cheese, cut into small pieces with the rind removed

salt and freshly ground black pepper

**TAPENADE**

¾ cup pitted black olives

1 garlic clove

2 tablespoons extra-virgin olive oil

1 tablespoon lemon juice

2 tablespoons chopped flat-leaf parsley leaves

1 To make the tapenade, put the olives and garlic in a food processor and process until coarsely chopped. Add the olive oil and lemon juice and process again to obtain a coarse puree. Transfer to a bowl, season with salt and pepper, and stir in the parsley.

2 Toast the pine nuts in a dry, heavy-bottomed skillet over medium heat 3 to 4 minutes, stirring occasionally, until light brown. Remove the pine nuts from the pan, then put 2 of the tortillas in the pan and warm them over medium-low heat, turning occasionally, about 20 seconds. Repeat with the remaining tortillas.

3 Spread 1 tablespoon of the tapenade down the middle of each tortilla and top with the spinach, red pepper, Dolcelatte, and pine nuts. Season with salt and pepper and roll up, tucking in the ends, then cut in half crosswise on the diagonal and serve.

# CHILLED ALMOND SOUP WITH FRUIT AND OLIVE KEBABS

A version of the classic Spanish *Ajo Blanco*, this chilled garlicky soup is served with a kebab of apple, olives, and grapes for dunking. In Spain, the soup is traditionally served as a first course at Christmas lunch.

**SERVES 4**

4 thick slices of white bread, crusts removed
1⅓ cups blanched almonds
3 garlic cloves, crushed
1 teaspoon salt
⅔ cup extra-virgin olive oil
3 tablespoons verjuice or white wine vinegar
1 green apple
1 tbsp lemon juice
16 green grapes
12 pitted green olives
ice cubes, to serve

1 Soak the bread in water 10 minutes. Meanwhile, finely chop the almonds in a food processor or blender. Add the garlic, salt, olive oil, verjuice, and 1 cup plus 2 tablespoons water.

2 Squeeze the bread in your hands to remove as much water as possible, then add it to the food processor. Process until smooth and creamy, then add another 1 cup plus 2 tablespoons water and process again. Cover and chill the soup at least 2 hours.

3 Just before serving, make the kebabs. Peel, core, and cut the apple into bite-size chunks, then toss in the lemon juice to prevent them from discoloring. Thread the apple chunks, 4 grapes, and 3 olives onto each of four skewers. Ladle the soup into four bowls (if it is very thick, add a little more water first) and add a few ice cubes to each portion. Top with a kebab and serve immediately.

# KOHLRABI, MANGO, AND HERB NORI CONES

If making sushi sounds daunting, these filled nori cones are a great starting point because they don't require any fiddly rolling or special tools. The softness of the noodles is a wonderful contrast to the crisp texture and slight heat of the kohlrabi and the sweetness of the mango.

**SERVES 4**

1 ¾ ounces vermicelli rice noodles

1 tablespoon ume plum seasoning
or rice vinegar

4 nori sheets, quartered

4 teaspoons wasabi paste

16 large basil leaves

½ mango, peeled, pitted, and cut
into strips

3 ½ ounces kohlrabi or turnip,
peeled and cut into matchsticks

2 scallions, sliced

a few sprigs of cilantro, leaves only

**PLUM DIPPING SAUCE**

¼ cup plum sauce

1-inch piece of ginger root, peeled
and cut into fine matchsticks

1 To make the dipping sauce, mix together the plum sauce, ginger root, and ¼ cup warm water in a small bowl, then set aside.

2 Put the noodles in a heatproof bowl and add enough boiling water to cover them. Stir to separate the noodles, then let stand, covered, 5 to 7 minutes until soft. Drain the noodles and refresh under cold running water. Return the noodles to the bowl, add the ume plum seasoning, and turn until coated.

3 To make the nori cones, smear a little wasabi diagonally down the middle of each nori square. Top with 1 large basil leaf, then with 1 tablespoon of noodles, leaving a little gap at the bottom of the nori to allow you to roll it up. Put a strip of mango, 4 sticks of kohlrabi, a little scallion, and a few cilantro leaves on top of the noodles. Take the nori sheet in your hand and roll into a cone shape. Wet the edge of the nori and press to seal. Repeat to make 15 more cones. Serve with the dipping sauce.

# VIETNAMESE TOFU AND MANGO SALAD CUPS

**SERVES 4**

9 ounces firm smoked tofu

16 large Little Gem lettuce leaves

1 mango, peeled, pitted, and cut into
   strips with a vegetable peeler

1 small cucumber, cut into thin,
   1-inch long slices

1 small handful of mint leaves,
   chopped

1 small handful of cilantro leaves,
   chopped

2 tablespoons coarsely chopped
   roasted peanuts

salt

### CHILI & LIME DRESSING

2 tablespoons vegetarian fish sauce

¼ cup lime juice

1 red chili, thinly sliced crosswise

1 small garlic clove, crushed

1 teaspoon granulated sugar

**1** To make the dressing, mix all of the ingredients together in a small serving bowl, and set aside.

**2** Pat the tofu dry with a piece of paper towel, then cut it into ½-inch slices.

**3** Arrange the lettuce leaves on a plate. Divide the mango, cucumber, and tofu onto the lettuce leaves, using each leaf as a "cup." Sprinkle with the mint and cilantro leaves, then spoon a little dressing over each one. Top with the peanuts and serve.

# AVOCADO AND BEET SALAD WITH HORSERADISH DRESSING

**SERVES 4**

2 tablespoons sunflower seeds

2 tablespoons pumpkin seeds

1 avocado

7 ounces mixed baby salad leaves

1 beet, peeled and coarsely grated

1 small handful of alfalfa and
   broccoli sprouts

### HORSERADISH DRESSING

2 tablespoons olive oil

1 tablespoon lemon juice

1 tablespoon apple cider vinegar

1 tablespoon creamed horseradish

1 tablespoon light cream

salt and freshly ground black pepper

**1** Toast the seeds in a dry skillet and over medium heat 3–5 minutes, stirring often, until slightly golden. Watch carefully so they do not burn. Remove from the heat and set aside.

**2** To make the dressing, whisk together all of the ingredients with 1 tablespoon warm water, season with salt and pepper, and set aside.

**3** Cut the avocado in half, remove the pit, and scoop out the flesh, then cut the flesh into small chunks.

**4** Line a serving plate with the salad leaves and top with the beet, avocado, and sprouts. Drizzle with the dressing, then sprinkle the toasted seeds over the top just before serving.

# MEXICAN GAZPACHO

Lime, cilantro, and tequila give this classic chilled soup a Mexican feel. For the best flavor, use perfectly ripe tomatoes—take a sniff, they should smell beautifully aromatic.

**SERVES 4**

2 slices of day-old bread, crusts removed
2 pounds 4 ounces tomatoes
1 cucumber, peeled, seeded, and chopped
1 red bell pepper, seeded and chopped
1 to 2 jalapeño chilies, seeded and finely chopped
2 garlic cloves
1 tablespoon chopped oregano leaves
2 tablespoons olive oil
1 to 2 tablespoons tequila
juice of 2 limes
salt
ice cubes, to serve

AVOCADO SALSA
1 avocado
1 teaspoon lime juice
½ small red onion, finely chopped
¼ cup cooked black beans
2 tablespoons chopped cilantro leaves

**1** Soak the bread in ⅔ cup cold water 5 minutes. Meanwhile, put the tomatoes in a heatproof bowl, cover with boiling water, and let stand 30 seconds, then drain. Peel, seed, and chop the flesh.

**2** Put half of the bread, tomatoes, cucumber, red pepper, chilies, garlic, oregano, olive oil, tequila, and lime juice in a food processor or blender. Add 1 cup plus 2 tablespoons cold water and process until combined but still chunky. Transfer to a large bowl and repeat with the rest of the ingredients. Combine the two batches and season with salt to taste. Cover and chill 2 to 3 hours.

**3** Just before serving, make the avocado salsa. Cut the avocado in half, remove the pit, and scoop the flesh out, using a large spoon. Cut the flesh into small cubes and put it in a bowl. Stir in the lime juice, red onion, black beans, and cilantro leaves.

**4** Ladle the soup into bowls, add the ice cubes, and top with a large spoonful of the salsa. Serve immediately.

# NOODLES WITH VEGETABLE SPAGHETTI AND MISO DRESSING

The success of this vibrant salad relies on slicing the vegetables into fine shreds, or julienne, so their flavors blend and take on the nuances of the miso dressing.

**SERVES 4**

8 ounces vermicelli noodles
1 tablespoon sesame seeds
1 zucchini
1 large carrot
3 ½ ounces daikon, peeled
1 ½ cups finely shredded red cabbage
5 scallions, finely sliced
1 heaped tablespoon nori flakes
1 handful of basil leaves, torn
1 handful of cilantro leaves, chopped
1 small handful of radish sprouts
salt and freshly ground black pepper

**MISO DRESSING**

3 tablespoons yellow miso paste
3 tablespoons rice vinegar
2 teaspoons light soy sauce
1 tablespoon sesame oil
2 tablespoons sunflower oil
1 teaspoon ground mustard powder
2 tablespoons very finely chopped
  peeled ginger root

1 Put the noodles in a heatproof bowl and cover with boiled water. Stir to separate the noodles and let stand, covered, 5 minutes, or until tender. Drain, refresh under cold running water, return to the bowl, and cover with cold water until ready to serve.

2 Meanwhile, toast the sesame seeds in a dry skillet over medium heat for 3 to 4 minutes, stirring often, until slightly golden. Watch carefully so they do not burn. Remove from the heat and set aside.

3 Slice the zucchini, carrot, and daikon into long, thin strips, or julienne, using a mandolin, Microplane, or paring knife.

4 To make the dressing, mix together the miso and vinegar, and with 1 tablespoon hot water until smooth. Stir in the soy sauce, sesame and sunflower oils, mustard powder, and ginger, then season with salt and pepper.

5 Drain the noodles and put them in a serving bowl. Add half of the dressing and, using your hands, turn until the noodles are coated. Add the zucchini, carrot, daikon, cabbage, scallions, nori, and half of the basil and cilantro leaves and toss well. Drizzle with the remaining dressing and serve immediately, topped with the remaining herbs, sesame seeds, and radish sprouts.

# STUFFED TOMATOES WITH CRUSHED BEANS, MOZZARELLA, AND CHIMICHURRI

Chimichurri is an Argentinian herb and garlic sauce, rather like pesto with an edge—it adds a simple, vibrant oomph to a dish. I've used canned legumes here, but you can soak and cook dried ones, if you prefer. Burrata, often referred to as the rich cousin of mozzarella, is a great, creamy alternative cheese to try here. Serve with crusty bread for mopping up the juices.

**SERVES 4**

4 beefsteak tomatoes

1 can (15-oz.) cannellini or navy
   beans, drained and rinsed

2 tablespoons extra-virgin olive oil,
   plus extra for drizzling

juice of 1 lemon

1 small red onion, diced

½ cup pitted black olives, coarsely
   chopped

6 ounces mozzarella cheese,
   drained and torn into chunks

2 zucchini, trimmed

2 tablespoons chopped mint leaves

salt and freshly ground black pepper

**CHIMICHURRI**

1 large handful of flat-leaf parsley
   leaves, finely chopped

2 large garlic cloves, crushed

½ cup olive oil, plus extra for
   drizzling

3 tablespoons sherry vinegar or red
   wine vinegar

2 teaspoons dried oregano

1 teaspoon ground cumin

½ teaspoon dried chili flakes

½ teaspoon salt

¼ cup chopped cilantro leaves

1 Cut off the top of each tomato and scoop out and discard the core and seeds. Put the tomatoes upside down on a plate and set aside to drain.

2 To make the chimichurri, mix together all of the ingredients in a bowl, then set aside.

3 Put the beans in a small mixing bowl and crush roughly with the back of a fork or a potato masher. Stir in the olive oil, lemon juice, red onion, and olives, then season with salt and pepper.

4 Slice off a sliver from the bottom of each tomato so they stand upright. Spoon the bean mixture into each tomato until filled nearly to the top. Divide the mozzarella over the top and spoon the chimichurri sauce over the cheese.

5 Using a mandolin or vegetable peeler, slice the zucchini into ribbons. Drizzle a little olive oil over the zucchini, then sprinkle with the mint and season lightly with salt and pepper Serve the zucchini on top of the tomatoes or alongside.

# FATTOUSH WITH LABNEH AND PRESERVED LEMON DRESSING

Labneh, a soft, creamy yogurt cheese, popular in the Middle East, is fun and easy to make at home—but you need to start a full day ahead. It's well worth experimenting when making labneh. Try flavoring it with crushed garlic, chopped herbs, or ground spices. For a quicker, softer cheese, reduce the draining time for the yogurt to 6 to 8 hours. You can also double the labneh recipe and roll tablespoons of the cheese into balls—you should have about 15. Put them in a sterilized glass jar, cover with olive oil, and keep in the refrigerator up to 1 week.

**SERVES 4**

1 large pita bread
6 tomatoes, halved, seeded, and cut into bite-size chunks
1 small cucumber, quartered lengthwise, seeded, and cut into bite-size chunks
1 large red bell pepper, quartered lengthwise, seeded, and cut into bite-size chunks
1 small red onion, thinly sliced into rings
¼ cup chopped mint leaves
¼ cup chopped flat-leaf parsley leaves
seeds from ½ pomegranate, separated (optional)

**LABNEH**
1 cup plus 2 tablespoons Greek yogurt
½ teaspoon salt

**PRESERVED LEMON DRESSING**
1½ preserved lemons
5 tablespoons extra-virgin olive oil
1 tablespoon lemon juice
½ teaspoon ground sumac or ground cumin
salt and freshly ground black pepper

1 To make the labneh, line a strainer with a piece of cheesecloth and rest it over a mixing bowl. Mix together the yogurt and salt and spoon it into the cloth. Draw the edges of the cloth up and twist the top to make a bundle, then let drain in the refrigerator about 24 hours, gently squeezing it occasionally to help the liquid drain.

2 To make the dressing, cut the lemon zest away from the flesh. Discard the flesh and finely chop the zest. Mix together the olive oil and lemon juice in a small nonmetallic bowl, then stir in the sumac and lemon zest and season with salt and pepper.

3 Slice around the edge of the pita bread to open it up and toast it in a dry skillet or under a hot broiler a few minutes until crisp. Let cool slightly, then tear into bite-size pieces.

4 Put the tomatoes, cucumber, red pepper, red onion, mint, and parsley in a large, shallow bowl. Add the dressing and toss to combine. Sprinkle the pomegranate and pita chips over the top.

5 Remove the yogurt from the cloth—it should now look like semisoft cheese. Crumble it into chunks and arrange on top of the salad, then serve.

# SAVORY CHEESECAKE WITH RED PEPPER AND CILANTRO RELISH

The finely chopped red pepper, chili, and red onion relish here add color, crunch, and plenty of zingy flavor, which is in sharp contrast to the mild creaminess of the savory cheesecake.

**SERVES 4 TO 6**

1 cup chopped roasted hazelnuts
$\frac{1}{3}$ cup cashew nuts
12 coarse oatcakes, broken
3 tablespoons butter, melted
1 $\frac{1}{4}$ cups cream cheese
scant $\frac{1}{2}$ cup ricotta cheese
$\frac{3}{4}$ cup finely chopped feta cheese
2 eggs, separated
2 teaspoons paprika
salt and freshly ground black pepper

**RED PEPPER AND CILANTRO RELISH**

2 red bell peppers, seeded and diced
2 green chilies, seeded and diced
1 small red onion, diced
1 large handful of cilantro leaves, coarsely chopped
juice of 1 lime

1 Put the hazelnuts and cashews in a food processor and pulse until finely ground. Add the oatcakes and process again to form fine crumbs. Transfer the mixture to a bowl, season with salt and pepper, and add the melted butter. Stir until combined, then press into the bottom of a loose-bottom, nonstick 8-inch round pan (you can also use individual pans if desired). Cover and chill 30 minutes.

2 In a large bowl, blend together the cream cheese, ricotta, feta, egg yolks, and half of the paprika and season with salt and pepper. In a clean bowl, beat the egg whites until they form soft peaks, then gently fold them into the cheese mixture. Spoon the batter into the pan and smooth the surface. Cover and chill about 2 hours, or until firm.

3 Mix together all of the ingredients for the relish and season with salt.

4 Remove the cheesecake from the pan, leaving the bottom, then dust with the remaining paprika. Cut into slices and serve topped with a good spoonful of the relish.

# APPLE, FENNEL, AND WALNUT SALAD

A mandolin might not be a must-have piece of kitchen equipment, but it makes slicing vegetables into paper-thin slivers incredibly easy.

**SERVES 4**

¼ cup walnut halves
2 tablespoons extra-virgin olive oil
2 tablespoons lemon juice
1 teaspoon wholegrain mustard
¼ cup sour cream
½ cup shredded red cabbage
1 small fennel bulb, thinly sliced
  lengthwise
1 green apple, thinly sliced
  horizontally, seeds discarded
2 tablespoons chopped flat-leaf
  parsley leaves
salt and freshly ground black pepper

1 Preheat the oven to 350°F. Put the walnuts on a baking sheet and bake 6 to 8 minutes until lightly toasted, then set aside to cool.
2 Meanwhile, in a small bowl, beat together the olive oil and lemon juice, then mix in the mustard and sour cream. Season with salt and pepper and set aside.
3 Put the cabbage, fennel, apple, and parsley in a mixing bowl, add the dressing, and toss well. Top with the walnuts and serve immediately.

# TURNIP, RADISH, AND DILL SALAD WITH MUSTARD DRESSING

This crunchy winter salad proves just how delicious most root vegetables are when served raw—just as good, if not better, than when cooked.

**SERVES 4**

5 ounces turnips, peeled
10 radishes, trimmed
5 ounces celery root, peeled and
  coarsely grated
2 tablespoons small capers, drained
  and rinsed
1 tablespoon chopped dill

**MUSTARD DRESSING**

5 tablespoons extra-virgin olive oil
2 tablespoons apple cider vinegar
2 teaspoons Dijon mustard
1 large garlic clove, peeled and
  halved
salt and freshly ground black pepper

1 Beat together all of the ingredients for the dressing and season with salt and pepper.
2 Slice the turnips and radishes into thin slices using a mandolin or sharp knife. Put them in a serving bowl, add the celery root, and toss to combine. Sprinkle the capers on top.
3 Remove and discard the garlic from the dressing, then drizzle it over the salad. Sprinkle with the dill before serving.

# SPROUTED BEAN, ARUGULA, AND PEA SHOOT SALAD

The nutritional value of legumes increases significantly when sprouted, providing about 60 percent more vitamin C. Most supermarkets carry a variety of sprouts, so experiment to find the ones you like best. They are also easy to grow at home in a sprouter, if you have one, or even in a jam or jelly jar (see page 15).

**SERVES 4**

¼ cup extra-virgin olive oil

2 tablespoons lemon juice

1 teaspoon Dijon mustard

3 tablespoons chopped garlic chives or ordinary chives

3 tablespoons chopped basil leaves

3 ounces arugula leaves

3 ounces pea shoots

1¾ ounces sugar-snap peas, trimmed and thinly sliced

1 small handful of mixed sprouted beans

1 small red onion, thinly sliced

salt and freshly ground black pepper

1 To make the dressing, beat together the olive oil, lemon juice, and mustard in a small bowl. Stir in the chives and basil and season with salt and pepper.

2 Put the arugula, pea shoots, and sugar-snap peas in a bowl and toss to combine. Top with the sprouted beans and red onion. Spoon the dressing over the salad and serve immediately.

# CRUNCHY ORIENTAL SLAW

**SERVES 4**

¾ cup shredded white cabbage

¾ cup shredded red cabbage

2 carrots, grated

4 scallions, finely sliced

3 tablespoons chopped mint leaves

3 tablespoons shredded basil leaves

SESAME AND GINGER DRESSING

1-inch piece ginger root, peeled and grated

2 tablespoons olive oil

4 teaspoons toasted sesame oil

2 tablespoons rice vinegar

salt and freshly ground black pepper

1 To make the dressing, squeeze the ginger in one hand to extract the juice into a bowl. Beat in the remaining ingredients and season with salt and pepper.

2 Put the white and red cabbage, carrots, scallions, mint, and basil in a bowl. Add the dressing and toss to coat. This slaw is at its best served at room temperature.

# CARAMEL, CHOCOLATE, AND MAPLE SEMIFREDDO

Gloriously simple, this creamy, maple-sweetened indulgence is decorated with frozen grapes. These might sound unusual, but they take on a whole new character when frozen, almost like mini fruit ice pops, and an attractive icy bloom.

**SERVES 8 TO 10**

3 eggs, separated

heaped ½ cup granulated sugar

2 tablespoons maple syrup

1¼ cups heavy cream

3½ ounces milk chocolate with toffee or caramel pieces, finely chopped

8 to 10 sprigs of seedless black grapes, to serve

1 Line the bottom and sides of a 9 x 5-inch bread pan with a double layer of plastic wrap, leaving enough excess hanging over the edges to completely cover the top of the semifreddo. In a large bowl, beat the eggs yolks, sugar, and maple syrup until pale and light. In another bowl, whip the cream until it forms soft peaks. In a third clean bowl, beat the egg whites until they form firm peaks. Gently fold the whipped cream into the egg yolk mixture, then gradually fold in the egg whites to make a light, fluffy mixture.

2 Sprinkle one-third of the chocolate into the bottom of the pan. Pour half of the cream mixture over the chocolate, followed by another third of the chocolate. Pour in the remaining cream mixture and sprinkle the rest of the chocolate over the top in an even layer. Cover with the excess plastic wrap and freeze 4 to 6 hours, or until solid.

3 Wash the grapes without removing them from the vine (you want 1 sprig per person) and put them on a baking tray. Freeze 1 to 2 hours or until frozen.

4 Remove the grapes and semifreddo from the freezer 10 minutes before serving. Unpeel the top of the plastic wrap, then turn the semifreddo out onto a serving plate. Peel away the rest of the plastic wrap and cut the semifreddo into slices. Top with the frozen grapes and serve immediately.

# VANILLA CHEESECAKES WITH BLACKBERRIES IN CASSIS

**SERVES 4**

1 cup blackberries

2 tablespoons crème de cassis
　　liqueur

1 cup cream cheese

1/3 cup confectioners' sugar

2 teaspoons vanilla extract

1/4 cup heavy cream

**HAZELNUT CRUST**

sunflower oil, for greasing

1/2 cup roasted chopped hazelnuts

1/2 cup jumbo rolled oats

2 teaspoons virgin coconut oil,
　　melted if solid

1 tablespoon agave syrup or
　　maple syrup

1 Put the blackberries and cassis in a bowl and let steep for at least 30 minutes.

2 Meanwhile, lightly grease four 2 1/2 -inch presentation rings and arrange them on a small baking sheet. In a food processor, grind the nuts and oats until the consistency of coarse bread crumbs. Add the coconut oil and agave syrup and pulse until combined. Divide the mixture into the rings and press down with the back of a teaspoon to make a firm, level crust. Chill while you make the topping.

3 Beat together the cream cheese, confectioners' sugar, vanilla extract, and heavy cream until thick. Spoon the batter over the cheesecake crusts and level the tops. Chill 1 hour, or until firm.

4 To serve, carefully run a knife around the inside of the rings to loosen the cheesecakes onto serving plates. Decorate the top of each cheesecake with the blackberries and spoon a little of the cassis over the top, then serve.

# RAW APRICOT AND ALMOND PANFORTE

Praised as one of nature's superfoods, raw cacao, or raw chocolate, is nutritionally potent. Combining it with nuts, seeds, and dried fruit in this recipe creates a delicious, healthy treat.

**MAKES 8**

1/4 cup coarsely chopped blanched
　　almonds

1/4 cup coarsely chopped toasted
　　hazelnuts

1/2 cup jumbo old-fashioned oatmeal

2 tablespoons pumpkin seeds

2 tablespoons sunflower seeds

1 cup ready-to-eat unsulfured dried
　　apricots, coarsely chopped

3/4 cup raisins

5 tablespoons freshly squeezed
　　orange juice

2 tablespoons raw cacao powder

2 tablespoons raw cacao nibs

1 Put the almonds, hazelnuts, oats, pumpkin, and sunflower seeds in a food processor and process until finely chopped. Transfer the mixture into a mixing bowl.

2 Put the apricots, raisins, and orange juice in the food processor and puree to a smooth, thick paste; you might need to occasionally scrape the fruit mixture from the side of the food processor bowl to get the right consistency. Scrape the fruit puree into the bowl with the nut mixture, add the cacao powder and nibs, and mix well.

3 Line a 10- x 7-inch baking pan with waxed paper or plastic wrap. Transfer the nut and fruit mixture to the pan and, using a metal spatula, smooth into an even layer about 1/2 inch thick. Chill 1 hour, then cut into 8 bars and serve.

# WATERMELON AND VODKA CRUSH WITH POMEGRANATE

Vibrant and refreshing, this "grown-up" granita is a great simple dinner party dessert. For a dramatic, modern look, freeze it in cone-shaped ice cream molds or a cone made from baking parchment paper.

**SERVES 4 OR 6**

3 pounds 5 ounces watermelon
1/3 cup granulated sugar
5 tablespoons vodka
1 tablespoon lemon juice
finely shredded zest of 1/2 lime
pomegranate seeds, to serve

1 Cut the watermelon into wedges, then cut away the black seeds and skin. Cut the flesh into chunks and puree in a blender. Press the puree through a strainer into a bowl, then add the sugar and stir until it dissolves. Stir in the vodka and lemon juice.

2 Pour into 4 or 6 cone-shaped ice cream molds or a 4-cup freezerproof container with a lid. Cover the cones with plastic wrap or the container with its lid, and freeze 3 to 4 hours until frozen.

3 Remove from the freezer about 15 minutes before serving to soften slightly, then gently slip the out of the molds, if using, or scrape the top with a fork and divide the ice crystals into glasses. Sprinkle with the lime zest and pomegranate seeds and serve immediately.

# MANGO KULFI WITH FRESH BERRIES

**SERVES 8**

1 large ripe mango, peeled and seeded
1 teaspoon vanilla extract
1 3/4 cups evaporated milk
1/4 cup sweetened condensed milk
sunflower oil, for greasing
2 tablespoons chopped unsalted pistachios
silver leaf, to decorate (optional)
2 cups mixed summer berries, such a blackberries, red currants, raspberries, and strawberries

1 Put the mango, vanilla extract, evaporated milk, and sweetened condensed milk in a food processor or blender and blend until smooth and creamy.

2 Lightly oil eight 2/3-cup dariole or pudding molds (you can also use a 4-cup freezerproof container with a lid). Divide the kulfi mixture into the molds or the container. Cover the molds with plastic wrap or the container with its lid and freeze 1 hour, then stir with a fork to break up any ice crystals. Smooth the top and return to the freezer. Freeze another 3 hours, or until frozen solid.

3 To remove the kulfi from the molds, take them out of the freezer 15 minutes before serving. Run a knife around the side of each one, then turn upside down and give the mold a little shake to release the kulfi onto a serving plate. You can also put the molds in a bowl of hot water for a few seconds to help release the kulfi.

4 Sprinkle the pistachios over the tops and decorate with a few flakes of silver leaf, if using. Serve immediately with the mixed berries.

## ORANGE-DRENCHED DATE AND RAW CHOCOLATE TRUFFLES

**MAKES 18**

⅓ cup blanched almonds

⅓ cup cashew nuts

heaped 1 cup ready-to-eat dried
  pitted dates, coarsely chopped

3 tablespoons orange juice

grated zest of 1 orange

1 tablespoon agave syrup or honey

3 tablespoons raw cacao powder, plus
  extra for coating

seeds from 2 or 3 green cardamom
  pods

½ cup shredded coconut, for coating

1 Put the almonds and cashews in a food processor and process until ground, then transfer to a mixing bowl. Put the dates in the food processor and process to a paste. You might have to stop occasionally to scrape the dates from the side of the food processor bowl. Put the date paste in the bowl with the nuts and add the orange juice and zest, agave syrup, and raw cacao powder.

2 Using a mortar and pestle, grind the cardamom seeds, then add them to the bowl. Stir until combined into a thick paste.

3 Coat a plate with extra raw cacao powder. Shape 1 tablespoon of the date and nut mixture into a ball and roll it in the cacao. Repeat to make 9 cacao-coated truffles in total.

4 Coat a second plate with shredded coconut. Follow the same method in step 3 to make 9 more truffles, this time rolling them in the coconut. Chill the truffles until ready to eat.

## SHRIKHAND WITH BLUEBERRIES

Sweet, creamy, and indulgent, this classic Indian dessert is made from strained yogurt and has a golden color thanks to the addition of saffron. For a quicker version, use Greek yogurt instead of plain and omit the draining stage. Simply mix the Greek yogurt with the cream and continue from step 2.

**SERVES 4**

2 cups plus 2 tablespoons plain
  yogurt

8 saffron strands

2 tablespoons warm milk

7 tablespoons heavy cream

¼ cup granulated sugar

1 vanilla bean, split and seeds
  scraped out

1 teaspoon cinnamon

1 ½ ounces dark chocolate

½ teaspoon freshly ground nutmeg

1 ¼ cups blueberries

1 Line a strainer with a piece of cheesecloth and rest it over a bowl. Add the yogurt, draw the edges of the cheesecloth up, and twist the top to make a bundle. Let drain 3 hours (or overnight if you have time) to drain the whey, gently squeezing it occasionally to help it drain.

2 Soak the saffron in the warm milk 15 minutes. Put the drained yogurt, cream, and granulated sugar in a mixing bowl and beat until thick. Stir in the vanilla seeds, cinnamon, and saffron mixture and divide into four small glasses or bowls. Chill 30 minutes.

3 Meanwhile, cut the chocolate into curls using a vegetable peeler. Sprinkle the chocolate and nutmeg over the shrikhand and serve with the blueberries.

## STRAWBERRY AND MARSALA SYLLABUBS

Marsala wine is the perfect match for strawberries and cream. The cream shouldn't be overbeaten but whipped until it forms soft, billowy peaks.

**SERVES 4**

1 pound 2 ounces strawberries, hulled

4 teaspoons confectioners' sugar

2 tablespoons granulated sugar

3 tablespoons Marsala wine or medium sherry

1 ¼ cups heavy cream

1 Reserve 4 strawberries for decoration and put the rest in a blender and puree until smooth. Press the puree through a strainer into a clean bowl to remove the seeds. Stir in the confectioners' sugar and set aside.

2 Put the granulated sugar, Marsala wine, and 1 teaspoon hot water in a large bowl and stir until the sugar dissolves. Add the cream and, using a balloon whisk, whip until it forms soft peaks.

3 Spoon a large spoonful of the strawberry puree into a small, tall glass or bowl and top with some of the cream mixture. Layer again with the remaining puree and cream. I like to use uneven layers for a more relaxed look. Chill the syllabubs 30 minutes until set. Decorate with the reserved strawberries and serve.

## PINEAPPLE SORBET WITH LEMONGRASS AND MINT CRUSH

This refreshing sorbet is perfect after a spicy meal. Beaten egg white gives the sorbet a light texture, but you can leave it out, if you prefer.

**SERVES 4**

1 large pineapple, peeled, cored, and cut into chunks, reserving any juice (heaped 3 cups prepared fruit)

¼ cup peeled and grated ginger root

3 tablespoons finely chopped preserved ginger in syrup, with 1 tablespoon of the syrup reserved

¼ cup granulated sugar

1 egg white

**LEMONGRASS AND MINT CRUSH**

1 handful of mint leaves, chopped

1 lemongrass stalk, finely chopped with outer leaves removed

⅓ cup granulated sugar

1 Put the pineapple and any juice in a food processor or blender and blend to a coarse puree, then transfer to a mixing bowl.

2 Using your hands, squeeze the grated ginger to extract the juice into the mixing bowl, discarding the pulp. Add the preserved ginger, reserved ginger syrup, and sugar and mix well. Pour the mixture into a sorbetière or 4-cup freezerproof container with a lid and freeze 2 hours.

3 In a clean bowl, beat the egg white until soft peaks form. Remove the mixture from the freezer and, if making by hand, stir with a fork to break up the ice crystals. Fold in the egg white, then return to the freezer and freeze 3 to 4 hours until frozen.

4 Remove the sorbet from the freezer 20 minutes before serving. Using a mortar and pestle, crush the mint leaves, then add the lemongrass and continue crushing until the mixture forms a coarse paste. Add the sugar and grind until well mixed. Serve the pineapple sorbet in scoops with the lemongrass and mint crush sprinkled over the top.

Broiling lends foods a rich, toasted flavor and draws out the natural sugars in many fruits, vegetables, and cheeses to add a slightly sweet, often caramelized note. From delicately browned frittatas and tortillas to crisp golden burgers and desserts, the recipes in this chapter exemplify the true versatility of broiling.

# BROIL

Warm Halloumi, Asparagus, and Fava bean Salad with Chipotle Dressing, page 58

# BLACK BEAN, JALAPEÑO, AND MOZZARELLA QUESADILLAS

**SERVES 2**

1 tablespoon olive oil, plus extra for
　brushing
1 red onion, chopped
1 garlic clove, chopped
1 red bell pepper, seeded and sliced
1 jalapeño chilli, deseeded and
　chopped
1 can (15-oz.) black beans, drained
2 large soft tortillas
2 ounces mozzarella cheese,
　drained and sliced
salt and freshly ground black pepper

1 Heat the oil in a large, nonstick skillet over medium-low heat and fry the onion 8 to 10 minutes until soft. Add the garlic, red pepper, and jalapeños and cook 2 minutes longer, stirring occasionally. Stir in the black beans and heat through, then roughly mash with a fork.

2 Preheat the broiler to medium-high and line the broiler pan with foil. Spoon the bean mixture on top of one of the tortillas, cover with the mozzarella and then with the second tortilla. Press the edges down slightly to encase the filling, then brush the top with oil.

3 Broil the quesadilla 4 to 5 minutes until golden and crisp, then carefully turn it over, using a metal spatula or pancake turner, and broil 4 minutes longer. Cut into wedges and serve hot.

# GOLDEN TOFU AND SMOKED PAPRIKA CORN SALAD

**SERVES 4**

2 ears of corn, husks removed
1 teaspoon smoked paprika
2 large handfuls of arugula
1 large handful of spinach leaves
3 cilantro sprigs, leaves only
3 mint sprigs, leaves only
4 tomatoes, seeded and diced
2 lavash flatbreads or tortillas

GOLDEN TOFU

1 tablespoon balsamic vinegar
1 tablespoon olive oil, plus extra
　for brushing
2 tablespoons honey
2 tablespoons tomato ketchup
1 tablespoons light soy sauce
9 ounces firm tofu, cut into 8 slices

DRESSING

3 tablespoons extra-virgin olive oil
1 tablespoon apple cider vinegar
1 small garlic clove, crushed
salt and freshly ground black pepper

1 To make the golden tofu, mix together the balsamic vinegar, olive oil, honey, ketchup, and soy sauce in a dish. Add the tofu and turn to coat, then let marinate at least 30 minutes.

2 Meanwhile, make the dressing. Beat together the extra-virgin olive oil and vinegar in a small bowl. Add the garlic and season with salt and pepper, then set aside.

3 Preheat the broiler to high and brush the broiler rack with oil. Brush the corn with oil, then dust lightly with the paprika. Broil 20 minutes, turning occasionally, until tender and blackened in places. Broil the tofu alongside the corn 20 minutes, turning once and brushing with more of the marinade, until golden.

4 Meanwhile, toss the arugula, spinach, cilantro, and mint together in a serving bowl. Add the dressing and toss well. Slice the corn kernels away from the cobs and sprinkle them over the salad, along with the tomatoes. Divide onto four plates and top each portion with 2 slices of the tofu.

5 Lightly brush the flatbreads with oil and broil 2 minutes, or until crisp, then sprinkle with salt and cut into wedges. Serve with the salad.

# TEMPEH TIKKA KEBABS WITH MANGO DIPPING SAUCE

Don't be put off by the long list of ingredients in this recipe—most are cupboard staples, and the tikka marinade can be whipped up in a few minutes. Tempeh is perfect for kebabs as it holds its shape during cooking and readily takes on stronger flavors, such as spices. If using wooden skewers, soak them in water 30 minutes before using, to prevent them from burning.

**SERVES 4**
14 ounces tempeh
²/₃ cup whole-milk plain yogurt
¼ cup mango chutney
heaped 1 teaspoon grated peeled
    ginger root

**TIKKA PASTE**
2 teaspoons ground coriander
2 teaspoons ground cumin
2 teaspoons turmeric
2 teaspoons ground ginger
1 tablespoon paprika
½ teaspoon cayenne pepper
2 tablespoons sunflower oil
3 garlic cloves, crushed
1 tablespoon tamarind paste
3 tablespoons whole-milk plain
    yogurt
salt

**RED ONION AND RADISH SALAD**
1 red onion, thinly sliced into circles
1 small cucumber, sliced into
    ribbons
8 radishes, sliced
lime juice, to taste
1 small handful of cilantro leaves

1 Steam the tempeh 10 minutes until slightly soft—this also removes any trace of bitterness. Remove it from the steamer and cut into 32 cubes, each about ¾ inch. Mix together all of the ingredients for the tikka paste and 2 tablespoons water in a large, shallow dish. Add the tempeh and turn until coated in the paste, then set aside to marinate at least 1 hour.

2 Preheat the broiler to high and line the broiler pan with foil. Thread 4 chunks of tempeh onto each of 8 skewers and broil 8 to 10 minutes, turning occasionally, until slightly blackened in places.

3 Meanwhile, mix the yogurt, mango chutney, and ginger together in a small bowl to make a dipping sauce and set aside.

4 To make the salad, arrange the onion, cucumber, and radishes in a shallow bowl and squeeze some lime juice over the top. Season with salt and sprinkle with the cilantro leaves. Serve the kebabs with the salad and dipping sauce.

## SMOKED CHEDDAR TARTINES WITH PEAR CHUTNEY

**SERVES 4**

4 thick slices of crusty wholewheat
  bread
1¼ cups grated smoked cheddar
  cheese
2 eggs, lightly beaten
2 teaspoons grainy mustard
salt and freshly ground black pepper
1 recipe quantity Pear Chutney
  (see page 180), to serve

1  Preheat the broiler to medium-high. Broil one side of the bread
   until toasted.
2  Mix together the cheddar, eggs, and mustard and season with salt
   and pepper. Spread the cheese mixture over the untoasted side
   of each slice of bread and arrange on a broiler pan. Broil 7 minutes,
   or until bubbling and golden. Serve the tartines with a good
   spoonful of the pear chutney.


## THAI TOFU CAKES WITH CHILI DIPPING SAUCE

**SERVES 4**

1 pound 2 ounces firm tofu, patted
  dry and coarsely grated
3 large garlic cloves, finely chopped
2 red chilies, seeded and finely
  chopped
2 lemongrass stems, finely chopped
  with outer leaves removed
2 kaffir lime leaves, finely chopped
1½-inch piece of ginger root, peeled
  and coarsely grated
4 scallions, finely chopped
¼ cup chopped cilantro leaves, plus
  extra to serve
1 large egg white
¼ cup all-purpose flour
salt and freshly ground black pepper
sunflower oil, for brushing

CHILI DIPPING SAUCE
¼ cup mirin
¼ cup rice vinegar
2 scallions, finely sliced
1 tablespoon granulated sugar
2 red chilies, seeded and finely
  chopped
3 tablespoons chopped cilantro
  leaves

1  In a small non-reactive bowl, mix together all of the ingredients for
   the chili dipping sauce and set aside.
2  Squeeze the tofu in your hands to remove any excess water and put
   it in a mixing bowl. Add the garlic, chilies, lemongrass, lime leaves,
   ginger, scallions, cilantro leaves, egg white, and flour. Season with
   salt and pepper and mix well. Shape the mixture into 16 tofu cakes
   of equal size, then cover and chill 30 minutes to firm up.
3  Meanwhile, preheat the broiler to high and line the broiler pan with
   foil. Brush each tofu cake with sunflower oil and broil 5 to 7 minutes
   on each side until golden, broiling in batches, if necessary. Sprinkle
   with extra cilantro leaves and serve warm with the chili
   dipping sauce.

# EGGPLANT, SCAMORZA, AND BASIL ROLLS

**SERVES 4**

2 eggplants, trimmed and each one cut lengthwise into 6 slices

7 tablespoons olive oil

3 tablespoons pine nuts

7 ounces scamorza (smoked mozzarella cheese), cut into 8 slices

4 large tomatoes, each cut into 4 slices

8 large basil leaves

balsamic vinegar, for drizzling

salt and freshly ground black pepper

1 Preheat the broiler to high and line the broiler rack with foil. Discard the outermost slices of eggplant and liberally brush the remaining ones with oil. Broil 12 minutes, turning once and brushing again with oil, if necessary, until tender and golden.

2 Meanwhile, toast the pine nuts in a dry skillet over medium-low heat, stirring occasionally, 3 to 4 minutes until light golden. Watch carefully as they burn easily.

3 Put 1 slice of scamorza, 2 slices of tomato, and 1 basil leaf in the middle of each slice of broiled eggplant and season with salt and pepper. Roll the eggplant over the filling and broil, seam-side down, 5 minutes, or until the mozzarella begins to melt and ooze out.

4 Serve with a drizzling of olive oil and balsamic vinegar and topped with the pine nuts.

# ARTICHOKE, TOMATO, AND BLACK OLIVE CROSTINI

Slicing the bread on the diagonal not only looks more attractive but you get a larger surface area for the topping. Rub the garlic over the toast while it's still warm—it literally melts into the surface of the bread, imparting a subtle flavor.

**SERVES 4**

1 small red onion, finely chopped

4 tomatoes, halved, seeded, and diced

16 pitted black olives, finely chopped

10 charbroiled artichoke halves, halved

2 tablespoons chopped flat-leaf parsley leaves

2 tablespoons chopped basil leaves

2 tablespoons extra-virgin olive oil

8 thick slices of ciabatta or similar open-textured bread

1 large garlic clove, halved

6½ ounces goat cheese, sliced

salt and freshly ground black pepper

1 Preheat the broiler to high. In a large bowl, mix together the onion, tomatoes, olives, artichokes, parsley, and basil. Add the olive oil, season with salt and pepper, and mix well.

2 Toast both sides of the bread under the broiler until light golden and crisp. Rub one side of each slice of bread with the cut side of the garlic, then top with the goat cheese. Broil 3 to 4 minutes until the cheese melts, then remove the crostini from the broiler.

3 Pile the tomato and artichoke mixture on top of the crostini and serve warm.

# WARM HALLOUMI, ASPARAGUS, AND FAVA BEAN SALAD WITH CHIPOTLE DRESSING

Halloumi is at its best when warm, so prepare it just before you serve this salad. Chipotles are smoked jalapeño chilies, and they lend a wonderful warmth to dishes. Here they are used in paste form, making a delicious smoky chili marinade and dressing.

**SERVES 4**

4 teaspoons chipotle paste

5 tablespoons extra-virgin olive oil

12 ounces halloumi cheese, patted dry and sliced

20 asparagus stems, trimmed

2 pounds fava beans, shelled

2 tablespoons chopped parsley leaves

3 tablespoons chopped cilantro leaves

4 handfuls of arugula leaves

1 small red onion, thinly sliced into circles

2½ ounces sun-blush tomatoes in oil, drained and halved if large

1 small garlic clove, crushed

2 tablespoons lemon juice

salt and freshly ground black pepper

1 Preheat the broiler to high and line the broiler pan with foil. Mix together the chipotle paste and 3 tablespoons of the olive oil in a shallow bowl. Add the halloumi and turn until coated, then set aside.

2 Brush the asparagus with 1 tablespoon of the remaining oil and broil 5 to 7 minutes, turning once, until tender. Remove from the heat and set aside, but do not turn off the broiler.

3 Meanwhile, boil the fava beans 3 to 5 minutes until tender, then drain and refresh under cold running water. Pop the beans out of and discard their outer shells, then put the beans in a bowl with the parsley and cilantro.

4 Divide the arugula leaves onto four plates and sprinkle the red onion and sun-blush tomatoes over them.

5 Remove the halloumi from the marinade and broil 3 minutes on each side, or until soft. Mix the marinade with the remaining olive oil, garlic, and lemon juice and season with salt and pepper. Pour it over the fava beans and toss well. Spoon the mixture over the arugula leaves, top with the halloumi and asparagus, and serve.

# BROILED MUSHROOMS WITH CHICKPEA MASH AND EGGPLANT SCHNITZEL

Broiling helps to seal in the mushroom juices, keeping them succulent and moist, while the combination of Parmesan cheese and matzo meal gives a crisp, crunchy coating to the slices of broiled eggplant.

**SERVES 4**

¼ cup olive oil

2 tablespoons balsamic vinegar

4 large portobello mushrooms, stems discarded

1 eggplant, cut lengthwise into 6 slices, discarding the outermost slices

½ cup finely grated Parmesan cheese

6 tablespoons fine matzo meal

salt and freshly ground black pepper

**SALSA VERDE**

½ ounce basil leaves, plus 4 extra leaves

1 large garlic clove, crushed

¼ cup olive oil

1 tablespoon lemon juice

**CHICKPEA MASH**

1 tablespoon olive oil

2 garlic cloves, crushed

2 cups cooked chickpeas

7 tablespoons milk

1 Preheat the broiler to high and line the broiler pan with foil. First make the salsa verde. Put the basil, garlic, olive oil, and lemon juice in a food processor and process until smooth. Season with salt and pepper and set aside.

2 Combine the olive oil and balsamic vinegar in a bowl and brush the mixture over the gills of the mushrooms. Broil, gill-side up, 5 minutes, then turn over and brush the caps with a little more of the oil mixture and broil 5 minutes longer, or until soft. Wrap the mushrooms in foil and set aside to keep warm.

3 Meanwhile, make the chickpea mash. Heat the olive oil in a pan over low heat and fry the garlic 1 minute. Add the chickpeas and milk, heat through and then remove from the heat. Mash coarsely and season with salt and pepper. Cover with a lid and set aside to keep warm.

4 Brush one side of the eggplant slices with the oil and balsamic vinegar mixture. Mix the Parmesan and matzo meal together on a plate and season with salt and pepper, then press the oiled eggplants into the crumb mixture. Broil, crumb-side up, 5 minutes, or until golden and crisp on the outside. Turn over, brush again with the oil mixture, and sprinkle with the remaining Parmesan and matzo meal until covered. Broil 5 minutes longer.

5 To serve, put 1 mushroom, gill-side up, on each of four plates and top with the chickpea mash. Fold each eggplant slice in half and put it on top of the mash. Top each eggplant with a basil leaf, then drizzle the salsa verde around the mushrooms and serve immediately.

# SPANISH EGG GRATIN

Smoked paprika is synonymous with Spanish cooking. Made from the ground dried pods of smoked red chilies, the spice lends a hot, rich smokiness to dishes.

**SERVES 4**

9 ounces spinach leaves, tough
   stems removed
2 tablespoons olive oil
1 large onion, chopped
2 large garlic cloves, chopped
1 red bell pepper, seeded and
   chopped
2 ½ cups tomato puree
1 tablespoon tomato paste
2 teaspoons dried oregano
1 to 2 teaspoons smoked paprika,
   to taste
8 eggs
heaped ½ cup grated sharp cheddar
   cheese
salt and freshly ground black pepper
2 tablespoons chopped parsley
   leaves, to serve

**GARLIC BRUSCHETTA**

7-ounce loaf of ciabatta, cut
   in half horizontally, then cut
   into quarters
olive oil, for brushing
2 garlic cloves, halved

1 Steam the spinach 3 to 4 minutes until it wilts and is tender, then squeeze out any excess water and set aside.

2 Heat the olive oil in a large sauté pan over medium-high heat and fry the onion 8 minutes, or until soft. Add the garlic and red pepper and cook 2 minutes longer. Stir in the tomato puree, tomato paste, oregano, and 1 teaspoon of the paprika. Taste and add the remaining paprika if you want a spicier sauce. Bring to a boil, then reduce the heat to low and simmer 10 minutes, or until reduced and thicker.

3 Preheat the broiler to medium-high. Spread the steamed spinach in an even layer in a large, shallow flameproof dish. Spoon the tomato sauce over the spinach and make 8 indentations in the top. Break an egg into each indentation, then broil 5 minutes, or until the eggs are almost cooked but the yolk remains runny.

4 Sprinkle the cheese over the top of the dish and broil 2 minutes longer, or until melted and golden.

5 While the gratin is cooking, heat a griddle pan over medium-high heat. Brush both sides of the ciabatta with olive oil and griddle in two batches about 8 minutes, turning halfway, or until crisp and golden. Rub the cut-side of the garlic over the toasted bread. Sprinkle the egg gratin with the parsley and serve with the garlic toast.

# POLENTA BRUSCHETTA WITH ROSEMARY, TOMATO, AND CANNELLINI BEANS

Polenta can be left to set, then cut into slices that are perfect for broiling. They take on a crisp texture and golden color and are a great base for toppings.

**SERVES 4**

heaped 1 cup instant polenta
3 tablespoons butter, diced
½ cup finely grated Parmesan cheese, plus extra to serve
1 teaspoon dried chili flakes
olive oil, plus extra for greasing and brushing
salt and freshly ground black pepper

**ROSEMARY BEANS**

3 tablespoons olive oil
4 large garlic cloves, chopped
2 tablespoons chopped rosemary leaves
2 cups cooked cannellini or navy beans
4 ounces sun-blush tomatoes, coarsely chopped
2 tablespoons lemon juice
3 cups baby spinach leaves

1 First make the polenta. Put 3½ cups plus 2 tablespoons water in a saucepan, then gradually stir in the polenta and bring to a boil. Reduce the heat to low and simmer, stirring, 8 to 10 minutes until thick. Remove the pan from the heat and stir in the butter, Parmesan, and chili flakes, then season with salt and pepper.

2 Lightly grease a baking tray with olive oil and spread the polenta into an even layer about ¾ inch thick. Smooth the top and let cool and set at room temperature

3 Preheat the broiler to high. Cut the polenta into 4 squares, then cut each square in half diagonally. Brush the triangles with oil, arrange them on the broiler rack, and broil 6 minutes on each side, or until crisp on the outside and golden in places. Work in batches, if necessary, keeping the broiled polenta warm while you finish making the rest.

4 To make the beans, heat the olive oil in a skillet over medium-low heat and fry the garlic and rosemary 30 seconds. Add the beans and sun-blush tomatoes and stir until heated through. Reduce the heat to low, stir in the lemon juice and spinach, and continue cooking until the leaves just wilt.

5 Serve 2 wedges of polenta per person, topped with the beans and sprinkled with extra Parmesan.

# SPICED KOFTA WITH APPLE AND MINT RAITA

Broiling gives these lightly spiced kofta a crisp, golden exterior, but they still remain moist inside. The heat of the accompanying ginger–tomato sauce is tempered by the cooling apple and mint raita.

**SERVES 4**
2 zucchini, coarsely grated
1 onion, coarsely grated
2 ½ cups cooked chickpeas
2 teaspoons ground cumin
2 teaspoons ground coriander
1 red chili, seeded and chopped
olive oil, for brushing
salt and freshly ground black pepper
1 recipe quantity Sesame Seed
 Naan (see page 72), to serve

GINGER–TOMATO SAUCE
1 onion, chopped
2 large garlic cloves, halved
2-inch piece of ginger root, peeled
 and chopped
2 tablespoons sunflower oil, plus
 extra for brushing
1 teaspoon fennel seeds
1 teaspoon dried chili flakes
1 ¼ cups tomato puree
7 tablespoons vegetable stock
2 teaspoons lemon juice
½ teaspoon salt

APPLE AND MINT RAITA
1 red dessert apple, cored, and
 coarsely grated
heaped 3 tablespoons chopped mint
 leaves
2 teaspoons lemon juice
½ cup plain yogurt

1 Squeeze the grated zucchini in your hands to remove any excess water. Put them in a food processor and add the onion, chickpeas, cumin, coriander, and chili. Season with salt and pepper and process to make a coarse, thick paste. Shape the zucchini mixture into 12 equal-size balls and chill 30 minutes to firm up.

2 Meanwhile, make the sauce. Clean the food processor, then process the onion, garlic, and ginger until smooth. Heat the sunflower oil in a pan over medium-low heat and fry the onion mixture, stirring occasionally, 6 minutes. Add the fennel seeds and chili flakes and cook 1 minute longer, then add the tomato puree and stock. Bring to a boil, reduce the heat to low, and simmer 10 minutes, or until thick. Stir in the lemon juice and season with salt and pepper.

3 Preheat the broiler to high and line the broiler rack with foil. Meanwhile, mix together all of the ingredients for the raita and set aside.

4 Brush the kofta with olive oil and broil 6 to 8 minutes on each side until golden. Warm the naan bread and put on four plates, add the koftas and ginger–tomato sauce. Serve with the raita.

# LEEK, APPLE, AND CHEESE SAUSAGES WITH WATERCRESS SAUCE

A version of the traditional Welsh Glamorgan sausages, these golden, crumb-coated ones feature grated apple and are served with creamy watercress sauce.

**SERVES 4**

4 cups fresh white bread crumbs

1 ½ cups grated sharp cheddar cheese

1 small leek, very finely chopped

1 dessert apple, cored and grated

1 teaspoon dried thyme

1 teaspoon Dijon mustard

2 tablespoons milk

2 eggs

olive oil, for brushing

2 ½ cups finely shredded savoy cabbage with the stems removed

2 tablespoons butter

2 teaspoons caraway seeds

salt and freshly ground black pepper

**WATERCRESS SAUCE**

5 ounces watercress, thick stems removed

2 tablespoons butter

3 tablespoons all-purpose flour

scant 1 ¼ cups milk

1 In a large bowl, mix 3 cups of the bread crumbs with the cheese, leek, apple, and thyme. Stir in the mustard, milk, and 1 of the eggs and season with salt and pepper. Shape into 12 equal-size link sausages and chill 30 minutes to firm up.

2 Meanwhile, preheat the broiler to high and line the broiler pan with foil. Beat the remaining egg in a bowl and dip each sausage in it, then roll in the remaining bread crumbs to coat. Lightly brush the sausages with olive oil and broil 12 minutes, turning occasionally, or until light golden and crisp on the outside.

3 Meanwhile, make the sauce. Blanch the watercress in boiling water 2 minutes, then drain and refresh under cold running water. Finely chop the leaves and set aside. Melt the butter in a heavy-bottomed saucepan over low heat, stir in the flour, and cook, stirring, 1 minute. Gradually beat in the milk, increase the heat slightly, and cook until thick, smooth, and creamy. Season with salt and pepper, then stir in the watercress and warm through.

4 Put the cabbage and 2 tablespoons water in a saucepan and cook, covered, over low heat 2 to 3 minutes, stirring occasionally, until just tender. Add the butter and caraway seeds, season with salt and pepper, and stir until the cabbage is coated.

5 Divide the cabbage onto four plates and top each portion with 3 sausages. Serve with a spoonful of the watercress sauce on the side.

# CASHEW AND CARROT BURGERS WITH PISTACHIO AND CHILI CHUTNEY

Far removed from the archetypal nut cutlet, these burgers have a light texture and slight Indian spiciness. The chutney adds just the right amount of piquancy and a delightful vibrant color.

**SERVES 4**

1 cup cashew nuts
1 tablespoon sunflower oil, plus
    extra for brushing
1 onion, finely chopped
2 teaspoons cumin seeds
2 teaspoons fenugreek seeds
1 teaspoon ground coriander
2 large garlic cloves, finely chopped
2 carrots, grated
1 cup fresh bread crumbs
1 egg, lightly beaten
heaped 1 tablespoon plain yogurt
all-purpose flour, for dusting
salt and freshly ground black pepper
1 recipe quantity Sesame Seed Naan
    (see page 72), to serve

**PISTACHIO & CHILI CHUTNEY**

¼ cup shelled pistachios
1 green chili, chopped
2 handfuls of cilantro leaves
2 handfuls of mint leaves
1 teaspoon granulated sugar
1 garlic clove, crushed
2 tablespoons peeled and grated
    ginger root
juice of 1 lime

1  Preheat the oven to 350°F. Put the cashew nuts on a baking tray and roast 6 to 8 minutes until light golden all over. Let cool.

2  Heat the sunflower oil in a skillet and fry the onion 6 minutes, stirring occasionally, until soft. Add the cumin and fenugreek seeds and fry 1 minute longer, then stir in the ground coriander.

3  Grind the cashew nuts in a food processor until finely chopped, then transfer to a mixing bowl. Add the onion mixture, garlic, carrots, bread crumbs, egg, and yogurt. Season with salt and pepper and mix well. With floured hands, divide the mixture into 4 equal pieces, then shape them into burgers and lightly coat in the flour. Chill 30 minutes.

4  Meanwhile, make the pistachio and chili chutney. Put the pistachios in a food processor and process until ground, then add the chili, cilantro and mint leaves, sugar, garlic, ginger, lime juice, and 3 tablespoons water. Season with salt and pepper and process to a smooth puree the consistency of mayonnaise, adding more water, if necessary.

5  Preheat the broiler to high and line the broiler rack with foil. Brush the tops of the burgers with oil and broil 8 to 10 minutes, turning halfway and brushing with more oil, until golden.

6  Warm the naan breads and split them open. Put a burger on one half, then top with a generous spoonful of the chutney. Cover with the other half of the naan and serve.

| BROIL

# SPICED POTATO CAKES WITH HALLOUMI AND PINEAPPLE RELISH

It's best not to over-boil the potatoes for these golden potato cakes—you want to cook them until they are slightly *al dente* and then let them dry thoroughly in the pan before grating. This will help them to hold together when forming into cakes.

**SERVES 4**

2½ pounds potatoes, peeled and quartered, if large
heaped 1 tablespoon cumin seeds
1 zucchini, grated
1 teaspoon turmeric
2 tablespoons butter, melted
all-purpose flour, for dusting
14 ounces halloumi cheese, drained and cut into 12 slices
large handful of arugula leaves
salt and freshly ground black pepper
alfalfa sprouts, to serve

**PINEAPPLE RELISH**

1½ cups diced pineapple
¼ cup chopped cilantro leaves
3 tablespoons chopped mint leaves
1 long red chili, seeded and finely chopped
2 tablespoons extra-virgin olive oil, plus extra for brushing

1 Cook the potatoes in boiling salted water 10 minutes, or until tender. Drain and let dry in the pan until cool enough to handle. Meanwhile, toast the cumin seeds in a dry skillet over medium-low heat, stirring occasionally, 2 to 3 minutes until light golden. Watch carefully as they burn easily.

2 Grate the potatoes into a bowl, add the cumin seeds, zucchini, turmeric, butter, and salt and pepper to taste, and stir until combined. Shape the mixture into 4 equal-size potato cakes, put them on a lightly floured plate, and chill 30 minutes.

3 Meanwhile, to make the pineapple relish, mix together all the ingredients in a bowl, season with salt, and set aside.

4 Preheat the broiler to high and line the broiler rack with foil. Lightly brush the foil with olive oil and put the potato cakes on it, then lightly brush the top of the cakes with oil. Broil 20 minutes, turning the cakes over halfway through and brushing with a little more oil, if necessary, until golden and crisp.

5 While the potato cakes are cooking, heat a griddle pan over medium-high heat until hot. Brush the halloumi with oil and then griddle it 2 to 3 minutes on each side until soft.

6 Put 1 potato cake on each of four plates. Top with a handful of arugula leaves, 3 slices of halloumi, and a spoonful of pineapple relish, then sprinkle with alfalfa sprouts and serve.

# VEGETABLE AND MOZZARELLA TORTAS WITH AVOCADO CREAM

Layers of broiled vegetables interspersed with creamy mozzarella make this a pretty, summery dish. Don't worry if you don't have presentation rings—you can simply layer the tortas on the plate for a more relaxed look. While this is an easy recipe to prepare, it does require some patience as the vegetables need to be broiled in batches. They can also be roasted in the oven.

**SERVES 4**

½ cup olive oil, plus extra for brushing and drizzling

5 tablespoons balsamic vinegar

3 zucchini, thinly sliced lengthwise

1 large eggplant, thinly sliced lengthwise, then each slice halved

1 large fennel bulb, thinly sliced lengthwise

1 red bell pepper, seeded and thinly sliced lengthwise

1 yellow bell pepper, seeded and thinly sliced lengthwise

4 seeded soft tortillas

2 x 4½-ounce balls of mozzarella cheese, drained, patted dry, and cut into 16 slices

1 handful of basil leaves

salt and freshly ground black pepper

**AVOCADO CREAM**

1 large avocado

1 tablespoon olive oil

½ to 1 teaspoon harissa paste

1 tablespoon lemon juice

1 tablespoon plain yogurt

1 Preheat the broiler to high and line the broiler rack with foil. Mix together the olive oil and balsamic vinegar, then brush the zucchini with the mixture. Arrange half of the zucchini on the broiler rack and broil 10 minutes, turning once, until golden in places and soft. Brush with more of the oil mixture, if necessary. Repeat with the remaining zucchini, then set aside, covered with foil.

2 Brush the eggplant with the oil mixture and broil in batches 12 minutes, turning once and brushing with more of the oil mixture, if necessary. Repeat with the fennel and peppers, broiling them 5 minutes on each side.

3 Meanwhile, make the avocado cream. Cut the avocado in half, remove the pit, and scoop the flesh into a blender. Add the oil, harissa paste, lemon juice, yogurt, and 1 tablespoon water and blend until smooth. Season with salt and pepper, add more harissa, if desired, then transfer to a bowl.

4 Heat a little of the olive oil in a large, nonstick skillet over low heat, then wipe with a crumpled piece of paper towel to remove any excess. Add 1 tortilla and cook about 5 minutes, turning once, until golden and crisp. Remove the tortilla from the pan and cut into wedges. Repeat with the remaining tortillas.

5 To assemble, put a 4-inch presentation ring on a serving plate and set aside 4 basil leaves. Layer the broiled vegetables and mozzarella inside, starting with a slice of eggplant, followed by pepper, basil, mozzarella, zucchini, more basil, fennel, more mozzarella, and more basil. Repeat with a second layer, then carefully remove the ring and top the torta with a basil leaf. Repeat to make 4 tortas. Drizzle the tortas with oil, sprinkle with black pepper, and serve with the avocado cream and tortilla crisps.

# SESAME SEED NAAN

**MAKES 8**

2 ½ cups all-purpose flour, plus
    extra for kneading
2 teaspoons granulated sugar
1 teaspoon salt
1 teaspoon baking powder
¾ cup milk
3 tablespoons sunflower oil, plus
    extra for greasing
3 tablespoons black sesame seeds
2 tablespoons butter, melted

1 Sift together the flour, sugar, salt, and baking powder into a large mixing bowl. Mix well and then make a well in the middle. Mix together the milk and sunflower oil and pour it into the well. Slowly incorporate the flour mixture from the edge of the bowl into the wet ingredients to make a soft dough. Turn out and knead 10 minutes on a lightly floured surface, adding a little more flour if the dough is too sticky. Put the dough into a clean, oiled bowl, cover with a clean, damp dish towel, and let rest in a warm place 35 minutes.

2 Meanwhile, preheat the broiler to high and put a large baking sheet on the upper shelf of the oven. Divide the dough into 8 equal balls and, on a lightly floured surface, thinly roll each one out into a large teardrop shape. Sprinkle with the sesame seeds, then press them into the dough with damp hands.

3 Broil 2 naans at a time 2 to 3 minutes, turning once, until puffed up and golden. Watch carefully so they do not burn. Brush with the melted butter and serve warm.

# WINTER ORANGE SALAD

**SERVES 4**

3 tablespoons pumpkin seeds
3 mandarin oranges, peeled and
    sliced into circles
1 tablespoon extra-virgin olive oil
1 tablespoon honey
3 ounces mixed salad leaves, such
    as watercress, red chard, and
    mâche
1 fennel bulb, thinly sliced
1 cup thinly shredded red cabbage

**LEMON AND MUSTARD DRESSING**

3 tablespoons extra-virgin olive oil
1 tablespoon lemon juice
1 teaspoon wholegrain mustard
salt and freshly ground black pepper

1 Preheat the broiler to high and line the broiler rack with foil. Toast the pumpkin seeds in a dry skillet over medium-low heat, stirring occasionally, 2 to 3 minutes until light golden. Watch carefully as they burn easily.

2 Arrange the mandarins on the broiler rack, brush with the olive oil, and drizzle with the honey. Broil 3 to 5 minutes until glossy and slightly blackened in places but still retaining their shape. Remove from the broiler and set aside to cool.

3 Meanwhile, beat together all of the ingredients for the dressing and season with salt and pepper.

4 Mix together the salad leaves, fennel, and red cabbage in a serving bowl. Drizzle the dressing over the salad and toss well. Arrange the mandarins on top, sprinkle with the pumpkin seeds, and serve.

## MIXED SWEET PEPPERS WITH CAPER AND HERB DRESSING

**SERVES 4**

1 red bell pepper, seeded and
   quartered
1 yellow bell pepper, seeded and
   quartered
1 orange bell pepper, seeded and
   quartered
olive oil, for brushing
1 small handful of basil leaves,
   to serve

**CAPER AND HERB DRESSING**

3 tablespoons extra-virgin olive oil
1 garlic clove, crushed
1 tablespoon oregano leaves
1 tablespoon capers, drained and
   rinsed
salt and freshly ground black pepper

1 Preheat the broiler to high and line the broiler rack with foil. Brush the peppers with olive oil and, working in batches, if necessary, put them on the foil and broil 10 to 12 minutes, turning once, until soft and blackened in places.

2 Meanwhile, beat together all of the ingredients for the dressing and season with salt and pepper.

3 As the peppers come out of the broiler, put them in a paper bag and let stand 10 minutes. This will make them easier to peel. Peel off and discard the skins.

4 Put the peppers in a shallow serving dish. Drizzle with the dressing and top with the basil leaves. Serve at room temperature.

## BROILED FENNEL WITH PANGRATTATO

Fennel's aniseed flavor can be very dominant when raw, but it takes on a softer, milder taste after cooking. Broiled until tender, the fennel goes particularly well with the crisp golden crumbs.

**SERVES 4**

3 fennel bulbs, thinly sliced
   crosswise
olive oil, for brushing
salt and freshly ground black pepper

**LEMON AND CHILI PANGRATTATO**

2 thick slices of slightly stale white
   bread, crusts removed
1 tablespoon olive oil
1 tablespoon butter
finely grated zest of 1 small lemon
1 small red chili, seeded and finely
   chopped

1 Preheat the broiler to high and line the broiler rack with foil. Brush the fennel with olive oil and broil 8 to 10 minutes, turning once, until tender.

2 Meanwhile, put the bread in a food processor and process into coarse crumbs. Heat the olive oil and butter in a skillet over low heat. Add the bread crumbs and fry, stirring frequently, 5 minutes, or until golden and crisp. Stir in the lemon zest and chili, season with salt and pepper, and then remove the pan from the heat.

3 Arrange the fennel in a serving dish, top with the lemon and chili pangrattato, and serve.

# LEMON MERINGUE TARTS

A twist on the classic lemon meringue pie, these individual tarts have a buttery, ginger cookie crust and are topped with a swirl of light meringue that is broiled briefly to give a touch of color—simply delicious.

**SERVES 4**

7 ounces ginger snaps

½ cup less 1 teaspoon butter, plus extra for greasing

½ cup lemon juice

2 teaspoons cornstarch

heaped ½ cup granulated sugar

1 extra-large egg yolk, lightly beaten

2 extra-large egg whites

1 Lightly grease four 3 ¼-inch loose-bottomed tart pans. To make the crust, pulse the ginger snaps in a food processor until they form very fine crumbs. Melt 5 tablespoons of the butter in a pan, add the cookie crumbs, and stir until combined. Divide the mixture into the pans and press to line the bottoms and sides. Chill 20 minutes to firm up.

2 Meanwhile, mix together the lemon juice and cornstarch in a saucepan. Add scant ⅓ cup of the sugar, then bring to a boil over medium-low heat, stirring continuously. Reduce the heat to low and simmer, stirring, 2 minutes, or until thick. Stir in the remaining butter and remove the pan from the heat when it melts. Spoon the lemon curd mixture into the cookie crusts, then return to the refrigerator and chill while you make the meringue.

3 Preheat the broiler to medium. Beat the egg whites in a clean mixing bowl until they form stiff peaks, then gradually beat in the remaining sugar to make a glossy, firm meringue. Transfer to a pastry bag with a plain tip and pipe the meringue on top of the lemon curd. If you don't have a piping bag, the meringue can simply be spooned on top of each tart and swirled into a peak.

4 Put the tarts on a baking sheet and broil 1 minute, or until the meringue is golden in places but remains marshmallowy and soft inside. Watch carefully as it can easily burn. Return to the refrigerator 20 minutes to cool and firm up the crusts again, then remove from the pans and serve.

# BROILED PLUMS ON BRIOCHE WITH LAVENDER YOGURT

This is the perfect pudding for when you are looking for something sweet and indulgent but don't have much time on your hands.

**SERVES 4**
10 plums, halved and pitted
2 tablespoons butter, melted
3 tablespoons dark brown sugar
½ teaspoon cinnamon
4 thick slices of brioche

LAVENDER YOGURT
½ cup Greek yogurt
3 tablespoons honey
a few dried lavender flowers

1 Preheat the broiler to high and line a baking sheet with foil. To make the lavender yogurt, put the yogurt in a bowl and drizzle with the honey. Sprinkle a few lavender flowers over the top and set aside.
2 Put the plums, cut-side up, on the baking sheet and brush with the butter. In a small bowl, mix together the brown sugar and cinnamon, then sprinkle the mixture over the plums. Broil 5 minutes, or until soft and caramelized in places.
3 Meanwhile, lightly toast the brioche.
4 Arrange the plums on top of the brioche and serve with the lavender yogurt.

# CARAMELIZED APPLE WITH CAMEMBERT ON WALNUT TOASTS

This simple, delicious dish is sure to appeal to those who can't decide between a dessert and a cheese course. It also makes a good light lunch served with a watercress salad.

**SERVES 4**
8 thick slices of walnut bread
3 tablespoons butter
3 tablespoons honey, plus extra for drizzling
4 red dessert apples, sliced crosswise into thin slices and seeds removed
6 ounces Camembert cheese, sliced

1 Preheat the broiler to high and line a broiler pan with foil. Toast both sides of the walnut bread until lightly toasted and golden, then set aside.
2 Meanwhile, heat the butter and honey in a small saucepan until melted, stirring occasionally. Arrange the apple slices on the broiler pan (you will probably need to cook them in 2 batches) and brush them with the honey-butter mixture. Broil 2 minutes on each side until soft and slightly golden.
3 Arrange the apple slices on the walnut toasts and top with the slices of Camembert. Broil a couple of minutes longer, or until the cheese is bubbling and golden in places. Serve 2 toasts per person, drizzled with extra honey, if desired.

# RASPBERRY CRÈME BRÛLÉES

The broiler has to be very hot before caramelizing the sugar topping on this French classic. Spraying a mist of water over the brûlées before broiling to encourage the caramelization process. A blowtorch is also great to use for this.

**SERVES 4**

1 ¾ cups heavy cream
3 tablespoons milk
1 vanilla bean, split lengthwise and seeds scraped out
heaped ¾ cup granulated sugar
5 large egg yolks
1 cup raspberries

1 Preheat the oven to 300°F. Put the cream, milk, and vanilla bean and seeds in a heavy-bottomed saucepan and bring to a boil over medium to medium-low heat.

2 Put heaped ½ cup of the sugar in a mixing bowl and set the remaining ¼ cup aside. Add the egg yolks to the mixing bowl and beat until combined, then add the cream mixture and stir until the sugar dissolves. Remove and discard the vanilla bean.

3 Divide the raspberries into four large ramekins and strain the cream mixture evenly over them. Put them in a deep baking dish and add enough hot water to come halfway up the sides of the ramekins. Bake 30 to 35 minutes until almost set—they should still be a little wobbly. Set aside to cool.

4 Just before serving, preheat the broiler to high. Sprinkle each brûlée with 1 tablespoon of the reserved sugar and spray lightly with a tiny amount of water to help it caramelize. Broil 4 to 5 minutes until the sugar forms a layer of golden caramel. Watch carefully as the sugar can easily burn. Let the crème brûlées cool 5 minutes to let the caramel become crisp, then serve. Or let cool completely and serve chilled.

# ALMOND AND AMARETTI PEACH CRUMBLES

**SERVES 4**

¼ cup blanched whole almonds
8 amaretti cookies
2 tablespoons butter, melted
2 tablespoons maple syrup
4 peaches, halved and pitted
whipped cream, to serve

1 Preheat the broiler to medium and line the broiler pan with foil. Lightly toast the almonds in a dry skillet over medium-low heat 2 to 3 minutes, tossing the pan occasionally. Take care as they burn easily. Let cool, then chop roughly.

2 Roughly crush the amaretti, then mix them with the almonds, melted butter, and maple syrup.

3 Arrange the peaches, cut-side up, on the foil-lined pan. Heap the amaretti mixture on top of each peach half, then broil 3 minutes, or until golden and beginning to crisp (they will crisp up farther as they cool). Serve warm with a generous spoonful of whipped cream.

This imaginative collection of delicious dishes draws on the many different frying techniques to give foods color, crunch, and flavor. From sizzling Asian stir-fries and crisp, deep-fried morsels to griddled bruschetta and irresistibly sweet treats, these recipes encompass a world of cooking.

# FRY

Cinnamon-Dusted Doughnuts with Chocolate Sauce, page 119

# PAN-PIZZA WITH CARAMELIZED ONIONS AND DOLCELATTE

This yeast-free pizza is fantastically simple. The crust is cooked on the stovetop, while the topping can either be raw, as in this southern Italian-inspired version, or browned under the broiler.

**SERVES 2**

2 tablespoons olive oil
1½ cups dolcelatte cheese, cut
    into bite-size pieces
2 tomatoes, seeded and diced
1 handful of arugula leaves
extra-virgin olive oil, for drizzling

**PIZZA CRUST**

1⅔ cups self-rising flour, plus extra
    for kneading
½ teaspoon salt
1 teaspoon oregano leaves
¼ cup olive oil
freshly ground black pepper

**CARAMELIZED ONIONS**

1 tablespoon olive oil
1 red onion, thinly sliced into rings
½ teaspoon light brown sugar

1 To make the caramelized onions, heat the olive oil in a nonstick skillet and fry the onion over medium-low heat 8 minutes, stirring frequently, or until soft and starting to brown. Stir in the brown sugar and cook, stirring, 3 minutes longer, or until sticky and golden, then set aside. Reduce the heat to low if the onions become too dark.

2 Meanwhile, make the crust. Sift the flour and salt into a mixing bowl and stir in the oregano. Make a well in the middle, add 2 tablespoons of the olive oil and 7 tablespoons water and mix, first with a metal spatula, then with your hands to shape the dough into a ball. Lightly knead the dough on a lightly floured work surface and roll it out to fit a 10-inch nonstick skillet.

3 Heat 1 tablespoon of olive oil in the pan over medium heat and spread the oil over the bottom, using a crumpled piece of paper towel. Put the dough in the pan and cook 5 minutes, or until light golden underneath.

4 Remove the pan from the heat, cover the pan with a plate, and carefully flip it over to release the pizza crust onto the plate. Pour the remaining tablespoon of oil into the pan, slip the pizza crust back into the pan, uncooked-side down, and cook 5 minutes longer until light golden.

5 Top with the caramelized onions, dolcelatte, and tomatoes and season with pepper. Add the arugula leaves, drizzle with a little extra-virgin olive oil, and serve.

# THAI-SPICED POLENTA WITH SWEET CHILI BOK CHOY

A fusion of flavors, this polenta, made with Thai spices, has an Asian twist.
Its soft, creamy texture is perfect with the crisp stir-fried vegetables.

**SERVES 4**
4 cups vegetable stock
1⅓ cups instant polenta
heaped 1 teaspoon Thai 7-spice
  powder
4 teaspoons butter

SWEET CHILI BOK CHOY
2 tablespoons sweet chili sauce
2 tablespoons light soy sauce
2 teaspoons sesame oil
2 tablespoons peanut oil
1 large onion, sliced
7 ounces long-stem broccoli,
  trimmed
2 bok choy, halved or quartered, if
  large, white part sliced and leaves
  left whole
3 ounces snow peas
3 garlic cloves, thinly sliced
1-inch piece of ginger root, peeled
  and grated
1 red chili, seeded and sliced into
  thin circles (optional)

1 Put the stock in a saucepan, gradually stir in the polenta, and bring
  to a boil. Reduce the heat to low and simmer, stirring,
  6 to 8 minutes until thick. Add the 7-spice powder and butter and
  stir until it melts, then cover with a lid and set aside.
2 Mix together the sweet chili sauce, soy sauce, and sesame oil and
  set aside. Heat a wok over high heat, add the peanut oil and fry the
  onion 2 minutes before adding the broccoli and white part of the
  bok choy. Stir-fry 2 minutes, then add the snow peas, garlic, ginger,
  chili, if using, and green leaves of the bok choy. Stir-fry 2 minutes
  longer, then add the sweet chili sauce mixture and toss well.
3 Divide the polenta onto four plates, top with the vegetables, and
  serve immediately.

# GIANT COUSCOUS WITH GOLDEN EGGPLANT AND HALLOUMI

Giant couscous, otherwise known as Israeli couscous, is becoming increasingly available in specialist food stores. The Lebanese grains are about the size of a small pea and retain their shape more successfully after cooking than the tiny-grained Moroccan variety.

**SERVES 2 TO 4**

1⅓ cups wholewheat giant couscous

1 teaspoon vegetable bouillon powder

5 tablespoons olive oil, plus extra for brushing

1 large eggplant, cut into bite-size cubes

2 tablespoons pomegranate molasses or date syrup

1 large onion, chopped

3 garlic cloves, chopped

2 zucchini, diced

1 large red bell pepper, seeded and diced

1 red chili, seeded and thinly sliced

1 teaspoon cumin seeds

2 teaspoons ras-el-hanout

5 ounces baby spinach leaves

2 tablespoons lemon juice

9 ounces halloumi cheese, patted dry and sliced

3 tablespoons chopped cilantro leaves

2 tablespoons chopped parsley leaves

salt and freshly ground black pepper

1 Put the couscous in a saucepan, add enough water to just cover, and bring to a boil. Stir in the bouillon powder, then reduce the heat to low and simmer, covered, 8 to 10 minutes until the stock is absorbed and the grains are tender but not mushy. Remove the pan from the heat and set aside, covered, 10 minutes.

2 Meanwhile, heat 3 tablespoons of the olive oil in a large, non-stick frying pan over medium-low heat and sauté the eggplant, stirring continuously, for 15 minutes or until softened and golden. Add the pomegranate molasses and stir until the eggplant is coated and glossy. Transfer to a bowl and cover to keep warm.

3 Clean the skillet, then heat the remaining oil and fry the onion over medium-low heat 10 minutes, or until golden. Add the garlic, zucchini, red pepper, and chili and fry 3 minutes longer, or until tender. Stir in the cumin seeds and ras-el-hanout, then add the spinach and cook 2 minutes, or until it wilts. Fluff up the couscous with a fork, then add it and the lemon juice to the skillet and mix well until heated through. Season with salt and pepper.

4 Heat a griddle pan until hot. Brush the halloumi with a little oil and griddle 2 to 3 minutes on each side until soft.

5 Top the couscous with the eggplant and halloumi, sprinkle with the cilantro and parsley, and serve.

# SOUFFLÉ OMELET WITH GOAT CHEESE AND ROSEMARY PESTO

For a perfect soufflé omelet, the egg whites must first be beaten to soft, light, fluffy peaks. This version is filled with melted Gruyère cheese and a pumpkin seed and rosemary pesto. Serve it with a green salad and crusty French bread.

**SERVES 2**
3 eggs, separated
1 tablespoon butter
½ cup soft goat cheese
salt and freshly ground black pepper

**PUMPKIN SEED AND ROSEMARY PESTO**
2 long rosemary sprigs, leaves only
1 large handful of basil leaves
1 garlic clove, crushed
5 tablespoons olive oil
¼ cup pumpkin seeds, lightly toasted
3 heaped tablespoons grated Parmesan cheese

1 To make the pesto, put the rosemary, basil, garlic, and olive oil in a blender or food processor and pulse until coarsely chopped. Add the pumpkin seeds and process again until finely chopped. Transfer to a bowl, stir in the Parmesan, and season with salt and pepper. Taste and add a little more oil, if necessary, then set aside.

2 In a bowl, beat the egg yolks with a fork and season with salt and pepper. Beat the egg whites in a clean bowl until they form soft peaks, then fold them into the egg yolks.

3 Preheat the broiler to medium-high. Melt the butter in a large, nonstick, flameproof skillet over medium-low heat, tilting the pan to evenly coat the bottom. Add the egg mixture to the pan and spread out with a spatula to cover the bottom of the pan. Cook 3 minutes, or until set and golden. Arrange the goat cheese over the omelet and broil 1 to 2 minutes until the cheese melts.

4 Remove the pan from the broiler and spoon a few small dollops of the pesto down the middle of the omelet. (The leftover pesto will keep for about 1 week in the refrigerator.) Carefully fold the omelet in half to enclose the filling, then cut in half crosswise and serve.

# JAPANESE ASPARAGUS EGG ROLLS

A Japanese omelet pan is rectangular, but you can also use a round pan to make these delicate, sushi-style vegetable rolls.

**SERVES 4**

1 tablespoon sesame oil

1 tablespoon mirin

12 asparagus spears, trimmed

2 tablespoons peanut oil

2 large shallots, finely chopped

5 scallions, shredded

2 red chilies, seeded and finely
  chopped

6 extra-large eggs, lightly beaten

a few sprigs of cilantro, coarsely
  chopped

salt and freshly ground black pepper

tamari soy sauce, to serve

pickled ginger, to serve

**PICKLED VEGETABLE SALAD**

5-inch piece of cucumber

1 carrot

3 tablespoons rice wine vinegar

1 tablespoon toasted nori flakes

1 tablespoon sesame seeds, toasted

1 To make the pickled vegetable salad, cut the cucumber and carrot into ribbons, using a mandolin or vegetable peeler. Put them in a bowl, mix in the rice wine vinegar, and season with salt. Divide the salad into four small serving bowls, sprinkle with the nori flakes and sesame seeds, and set aside.

2 In a shallow dish, mix together the sesame oil and mirin, then add the asparagus and turn until coated. Heat a wok over high heat and stir-fry the asparagus 3 minutes, or until tender. Remove from the wok and set aside.

3 Pour half the peanut oil into the wok and add the shallots, three-quarters of the scallions, and half of the chilies. Stir-fry 1 minute, then remove from the wok and set aside.

4 Season the eggs with salt and pepper. Heat a Japanese omelet pan or a medium, nonstick skillet with a little of the remaining oil over medium-low heat. Add a quarter of the beaten egg and swirl it around to evenly cover the bottom of the pan. Cook 1 to 2 minutes until set, then slide it out onto a plate. Cover to keep warm and set aside while you make 3 more omelets, adding more oil to the pan as necessary.

5 Trim each omelet into a square, if necessary, and spoon one-quarter of the shallot mixture down the middle of each one. Arrange 3 asparagus spears on top, then roll up the omelets and cut each roll into 1-inch pieces.

6 Divide the omelet rolls onto four plates, standing them up on their ends. Sprinkle with the reserved scallions, chili, and cilantro and serve warm or at room temperature with tamari for dipping and pickled ginger and vegetables as accompaniments.

# BLINIS WITH EGGPLANT CAVIAR AND HONEY FIGS

Just a smidgeon of oil is needed to fry these large blinis—you want the outside golden and crisp and the inside to remain light and fluffy. You can, of course, also make bite-size blinis and serve them topped in the same way as canapés.

**SERVES 4**

3 tablespoons pine nuts
3 figs, sliced lengthwise
honey, for brushing
sunflower oil, for frying
1 recipe quantity Eggplant Caviar
    (see page 222)
watercress, to serve

**BLINI**

2/3 cup all-purpose flour
1/3 cup buckwheat flour
1/2 teaspoon salt, plus extra
    to season
1 teaspoon active dry yeast
1/2 cup milk
5 tablespoons sour cream
1 egg, separated

1 To make the blini batter, sift both flours into a mixing bowl and stir in the salt and yeast. Mix together the milk and sour cream in a small saucepan and heat gently until lukewarm—make sure it is not too hot or the yeast will die. Remove the pan from the heat, beat in the egg yolk, then gradually stir the milk mixture into the dry ingredients to make a smooth, thick batter. Cover with a clean dish towel and let rest in a warm place 30 to 45 minutes until bubbles appear on the surface.

2 Meanwhile, toast the pine nuts in a nonstick skillet over medium-low heat 2 to 3 minutes until light golden, then set aside. Watch carefully as they burn easily.

3 Lightly oil the skillet and cook the figs over medium-low heat 1 minute on each side, then reduce the heat to low, brush the figs with honey, and cook 1 to 2 minutes longer on each side until golden and crisp.

4 When the batter is ready, beat the egg white in a clean bowl until it forms soft peaks, then fold it into the batter. Heat a lightly oiled, large nonstick skillet over medium heat. For each blini, add 1/2 cup of the batter to the pan and cook 2 minutes on each side until golden, reducing the heat if the blinis brown too quickly. (You might have some leftover batter.) Alternatively, make smaller blinis and cook them 1 minute on each side.

5 Top each blini with a large spoonful of the eggplant caviar, followed by a few slices of fig. Sprinkle with the pine nuts and serve with watercress.

# SPICED PEAR AND PECAN SALAD WITH POLENTA CROUTONS

For the best results, use slightly underripe pears so they retain their shape when frying them in the spiced-honey glaze. This substantial salad is a fabulous combination of color, flavor, and texture.

**SERVES 4**

2 tablespoons butter

2 slightly underripe pears, peeled, each cut into 8 wedges, and cored

1 teaspoon ground ginger

2 teaspoons honey

5 ounces arugula leaves

3 ounces watercress

½ cup pecans, toasted

3 ounces dolcelatte cheese, cut into bite-size pieces

**DRESSING**

¼ cup extra-virgin olive oil

1 tablespoon lemon juice

2 teaspoons Dijon mustard

salt and freshly ground black pepper

**POLENTA CROUTONS**

½ cup instant polenta

4 teaspoons butter

1 large pinch dried chili flakes

2 tablespoons olive oil, plus extra for greasing

**1** First make the polenta croutons. Put 1¼ cups water in a saucepan and sprinkle in the polenta, then bring to a boil, stirring frequently. Reduce the heat to low and simmer 6 to 8 minutes until thick. Remove the pan from the heat, stir in the butter and chili, and season with salt and pepper. Lightly grease a medium baking pan and spread out the polenta to about ½ inch thick. Smooth the top and chill until set, then cut the polenta into ½-inch cubes.

**2** Heat half of the olive oil over medium-high heat in a large, nonstick skillet. Fry half of the polenta croutons 12 to 15 minutes, turning regularly, until crisp all over, then drain on paper towels. Repeat with the remaining oil and croutons, then set aside.

**3** Wipe the pan with paper towels and melt the butter over medium-low heat, then fry the pears 3 to 5 minutes, turning once. Add the ginger and honey, turn the pears to coat in the mixture, and cook 1 minute longer until golden.

**4** Mix together all of the ingredients for the dressing and season to taste with salt and pepper. Divide the arugula and watercress onto four plates and drizzle with the dressing. Sprinkle the pecans over the leaves and top with the pears, dolcelatte, and polenta croutons, then serve.

# AKOORI WITH POTATO AND MUSTARD SEED PARATHA

Akoori, traditional Indian scrambled eggs, is flavored with chili, ginger, and cilantro. As with any version of scrambled eggs, the secret is not to overcook it or the eggs become tough and rubbery.

**SERVES 4**

¼ cup butter
1 teaspoon cumin seeds
4 scallions, thinly sliced
1 green chili, seeded and chopped
1 red bell pepper, seeded and diced
1-inch piece of ginger root, peeled and finely chopped
8 large eggs, lightly beaten
3 tomatoes, peeled, seeded, and diced
2 tablespoons chopped cilantro leaves
freshly ground black pepper

POTATO AND MUSTARD SEED PARATHA
scant 1½ cups all-purpose flour, plus extra for kneading
½ teaspoon salt, plus extra to season
2 tablespoons sunflower oil, plus extra for greasing
4 ounces potatoes, peeled and quartered, if large
1 small onion, finely chopped
2 teaspoons black mustard seeds
½ teaspoon ground turmeric

1 To make the paratha, sift the flour and salt into a mixing bowl, stir well, and then make a well in the middle. Pour ½ cup lukewarm water and half of the sunflower oil into the well and stir with a fork until combined, then use your hands to shape the mixture into a ball of soft dough. It should be fairly sticky. Add a little extra water if the dough is too dry.

2 Turn out the dough and knead on a lightly floured work surface 5 minutes until smooth, then transfer to a lightly greased mixing bowl, cover with a damp dish towel, and let rest 30 minutes. Meanwhile, boil the potatoes until tender, then drain and mash and set aside to cool.

3 Heat a skillet over medium heat. Add the remaining sunflower oil, reduce the heat to medium-low, and fry the onion 6 minutes, stirring occasionally, until soft. Add the mustard seeds and cook 2 minutes longer, then stir in the turmeric. Add to the potato and mix well to form a thick paste.

4 Divide the dough into equal 4 pieces and roll out 1 piece on a lightly floured surface into a ½-inch-thick circle. Spread 2 teaspoons of the potato mixture over one half of the dough, fold into a semicircle and then into quarters. Roll out again to about 8 inches in diameter and stretch into a teardrop shape. Pat off any excess flour and set the paratha aside while you repeat with the remaining dough and filling.

5 Heat a large, nonstick skillet over medium-low heat. Brush one side of a paratha with oil and cook, oiled-side down, 2 minutes. Brush the top with a little more oil, turn over, and cook 2 minutes longer, or until light golden. Wrap in foil and keep warm while you cook the remaining parathas.

6 To make the akoori, melt the butter in a nonstick skillet over medium-low heat. Add the cumin seeds, scallions, chili, red pepper, and ginger and stir-fry 1 minute. Season the eggs with salt and pepper and pour them into the pan. Using a spatula, gently stir 3 minutes, or until the eggs are scrambled but still creamy, then gently stir in the tomatoes. Spoon the akoori over the paratha, sprinkle with cilantro, and serve immediately.

# THAI FRIED RICE WITH CRISP GINGER

Jasmine rice, with its soft, yielding texture and unassuming flavor, readily takes on the fragrant notes of lemongrass, ginger, and chili. For the best results, make sure the cooked rice is completely cool before stir-frying and the grains are as separated as possible.

**SERVES 4**

1 ¾ cups Jasmine rice, rinsed
scant ½ cup sunflower oil
¼ cup peeled and grated ginger root
¼ cup toasted unsalted peanuts,
 brown skins rubbed off
2 teaspoons kecap manis
1 tablespoon vegetarian fish sauce
2 tablespoons light soy sauce
2 teaspoons lime juice
½ teaspoon granulated sugar
6 scallions, sliced diagonally
4 garlic cloves, chopped
1 long red chili, seeded and sliced
2 lemongrass sticks, finely chopped
 with outer leaves removed
a few cilantro sprigs, leaves only

1 Put the rice in a saucepan and cover with cold water by about ½ inch. Bring to a boil, then reduce the heat to low. Simmer, covered, 10 minutes, or until the rice is tender and the water is absorbed. Remove the pan from the heat and let stand, covered, 5 minutes. Spread the rice out on a baking tray and let cool completely.

2 In a wok, heat the sunflower oil to 350°F. Add half of the ginger and deep-fry 2 minutes, or until crisp and golden. Scoop out, using a slotted spoon, and drain on paper towels.

3 In a bowl, mix together the peanuts and kecap manis. Spoon 1 tablespoon of the oil from the wok into a skillet, add the peanuts, and fry over medium-low heat for 2 minutes, turning once, until dark golden and sticky. Watch carefully as the nuts burn easily. If they are becoming too dark, reduce the heat to low. Remove the pan from the heat and set aside. Mix together the vegetarian fish sauce, soy sauce, lime juice, and sugar in a bowl and set aside.

4 Pour off all but 3 tablespoons of the oil from the wok. Add the remaining ginger, the white part of the scallions, garlic, chili, and lemongrass and stir-fry over high heat 1 minute. Stir in the cold rice, breaking up any lumps. Add the fish sauce mixture and stir-fry until hot. Divide the rice between four bowls and sprinkle with the green part of the scallions, peanuts, and cilantro leaves. Top with a pile of crispy ginger and serve.

# STOVETOP SQUASH BISCUITS WITH CAVOLO NERO IN CIDER SAUCE

**SERVES 4**

heaped 2 cups peeled and seeded
   butternut squash cut into
   bite-size pieces
1 ½ cups all-purpose flour
½ teaspoon salt
½ teaspoon baking soda
1 teaspoon baking powder
5 tablespoons butter
1 extra-large egg, lightly beaten
2 tablespoons milk
3 tablespoons olive oil
2 leeks, sliced
12 ounces cavolo nero, sliced
   crosswise into thin strips
1 tablespoon thyme leaves
1 ½ cups cooked great Northern
   beans
1 cup dry hard cider
1 teaspoon Dijon mustard
¼ cup heavy cream
salt and freshly ground black pepper
leaves from a few parsley sprigs
   chopped

1 Steam the squash until tender, then transfer to a bowl, mash with a fork, and set aside to cool.

2 Preheat the oven to 150°F. Sift the flour, salt, baking soda, and baking powder into a mixing bowl. Melt 3 tablespoons plus 1 teaspoon of the butter and stir it into the dry ingredients, along with the mashed squash, egg, and milk. Stir to make a soft dough.

3 Heat 1 tablespoon of the oil in a large, nonstick skillet over medium-low heat. Spoon one-quarter of the dough into the pan and, using a spatula, flatten into a ½-inch-thick circle. Repeat to add another biscuit to the pan, reduce the heat to medium-low, and cook 4 to 5 minutes on each side until golden. Reduce the heat to low if the biscuits are browning too quickly. Transfer to an ovenproof plate, cover with foil, and keep warm in the oven while you cook the remaining 2 biscuits, adding another spoonful of oil to the pan. Keep the biscuits warm while you make the sauce.

4 Heat the remaining oil and butter in a large skillet over medium-low heat. Fry the leeks 4 minutes, stirring occasionally, then add the cavolo nero and thyme and cook, stirring occasionally, 3 minutes longer. Stir in the beans and cider, then increase the heat to medium-high. Cook 5 to 10 minutes until the cider reduce by half. Reduce the heat to medium-low and stir in the mustard and cream. Season with salt and pepper and warm through. Serve the biscuits with the sauce and sprinkled with the parsley.

# BARLEY WITH GARLIC, WATERCRESS, AND MELTING CAMEMBERT

**SERVES 4**

1 ¼ cups pearl barley
2 tablespoons olive oil
2 large garlic cloves, coarsely
   chopped
2 teaspoons dried oregano
1 long red chili, chopped
5 ounces watercress
1 to 2 tablespoons lemon juice,
   to taste
7 ounces Camembert cheese, rind
   discarded and cheese cut into
   bite-size chunks
salt and freshly ground black pepper

1 Put the barley in a saucepan, cover with at least 3 cups water, and bring to the boil. Reduce the heat to low and simmer, covered, 25 minutes, or until the grains are tender. Drain the barley and set aside.

2 Heat the oil in a large, nonstick skillet over low to medium heat and fry the garlic, oregano, and chili 1 minute. Add the barley and stir until it is coated in the oil. Stir in the watercress and lemon juice and cook 2 to 3 minutes until it wilts. Add the Camembert and cook, stirring, it melts and the mixture is warmed through. Season with salt and pepper and serve.

# YAKISOBA WITH TOFU AND GOLDEN CASHEWS

Yakisoba simply means stir-fried noodles, and this classic dish is bursting with fresh Asian flavors. A properly made stir-fry should be piping hot, with the vegetables cooked through but still crunchy. Have all the ingredients measured and prepared before you start to cook, that way it takes only minutes from wok to plate.

**SERVES 4**

2 tablespoons tamari soy sauce
1 tablespoon sesame oil
6 tablespoons teriyaki sauce
12 ounces tofu, patted dry and cut
    into ⅝-inch cubes
¼ cup cashew nuts
1 tablespoon kecap manis
12 ounces soba noodles
9 ounces long-stemmed broccoli,
    ends trimmed
3 tablespoons sunflower oil
1 large yellow bell pepper, seeded
    and cut into strips
2 garlic cloves, finely chopped
1-inch piece ginger root, peeled and
    finely sliced
8 scallions, sliced diagonally
freshly ground black pepper
2 tablespoons pink pickled ginger,
    to serve

1 In a shallow bowl, mix together the tamari, sesame oil, and teriyaki sauce. Add the tofu and turn to coat, then let marinate at least 1 hour.

2 Toast the cashew nuts in a dry skillet over medium-low heat 2–3 minutes, stirring occasionally, until golden. Transfer to a bowl, add the kecap manis, and stir to coat the nuts. Return the nuts to the skillet and cook 1 minute, turning once, until golden and glossy. Watch carefully as they can easily burn. Remove the nuts from the pan, spread them out on a baking sheet and let cool.

3 Cook the soba noodles according to the package directions, adding the broccoli 2 minutes before the end of the cooking time. Drain and refresh under cold running water.

4 Heat a large wok over high heat. Add 2 tablespoons of the sunflower oil and fry the tofu over medium heat, reserving the marinade, 8 to 10 minutes, turning occasionally, until golden. Remove from the wok and set aside, covered.

5 Wipe the wok with paper towels, then heat the remaining sunflower oil over medium heat. Add the yellow pepper, garlic, ginger, and the white part of the scallions and stir well. Turn the heat down to medium-low and add the broccoli, noodles, and reserved marinade. Stir until combined and warmed through, then season with pepper. Divide between four large, shallow bowls. Top with the tofu, nuts, the green part of the scallions, and the pickled ginger, then serve.

# CARROT–POTATO RÖSTI WITH EGG AND CARAMELIZED TOMATOES

**SERVES 4**

1 pound 7 ounces potatoes, peeled
(about 6)

2 carrots, peeled and grated

5 tablespoons olive oil, for frying,
plus extra if needed

4 eggs

salt and freshly ground black pepper

**CARAMELIZED TOMATOES**

2 tablespoons olive oil

12 ounces cherry tomatoes, halved

4 thyme sprigs, leaves only

2 tablespoons balsamic vinegar

1 Boil the potatoes in salted water 8 to 10 minutes until tender, then drain and let cool. Once cool, grate into a mixing bowl and add the carrots. Season with salt and pepper, mix well, and shape into 8 rösti, each about 2¾ inches diameter and 1 inch thick.

2 Preheat the oven to 150°F. In a large, nonstick skillet, heat 3 tablespoons of the olive oil over medium heat. Working in batches, fry the rösti 6 minutes on each side, or until crisp, reducing the heat to medium low if they start to cook too quickly. Drain on paper towels, then cover with foil and keep warm in the oven while you make the remaining rösti. Add more oil to the pan, if needed.

3 To make the caramelized tomatoes, heat the olive oil in a skillet over medium-low heat and add the tomatoes and half of the thyme. Cook 1 minute, turning the tomatoes once, then add the balsamic vinegar. Reduce the heat to low and cook 2 minutes, turning occasionally, until the tomatoes start to caramelize. Season to taste with salt and pepper and set aside.

4 To fry the eggs, add the remaining 2 tablespoons of the oil to the cleaned skillet, if necessary. Crack the eggs into the pan and fry over medium-low heat 4 minutes until the whites are cooked but the yolks are still runny. Serve 2 rösti per person, topped with 1 fried egg, sprinkled with the remaining thyme, and served with the tomatoes.

# ORANGE AND TAMARI-GLAZED TEMPEH

**SERVES 4**

juice of 3 oranges

3 tablespoons honey

3 tablespoons tamari soy sauce

¼ teaspoon dried chili flakes
(optional)

cornstarch, for dusting

14 ounces tempeh, patted dry and
cut into ¼-inch slices

½ cup sunflower oil

cooked rice, to serve

1 Mix together the orange juice, honey, tamari, and chili flakes, if using, then set aside.

2 Cover a small plate with cornstarch. Dip both sides of each slice of tempeh into the cornstarch to lightly coat.

3 Heat the sunflower oil in a large skillet over medium heat. Add half of the tempeh and fry 8 to 10 minutes, turning once, until crisp and light golden. Remove the tempeh from the pan and drain on paper towels. Repeat with the remaining tempeh.

4 Drain the oil from the pan and return half of the tempeh. Add half of the orange juice mixture and cook over medium-low heat 2 minutes, turning once, until the liquid thickens and the tempeh is glossy and golden. Keep warm while you cook the remaining tempeh. Serve hot with rice.

# BLACK BEAN VEGETABLES WITH CRISP NOODLE NESTS

**SERVES 4**

3 tablespoons Chinese black beans

2 tablespoons soy sauce

1 teaspoon cornstarch

1½ cups sunflower oil, for
   deep-frying

3½ oz of dry vermicelli rice noodles

10 ounces long-stemmed broccoli,
   stems sliced and florets left whole

1 large yellow bell pepper, seeded
   and sliced

6 scallions, sliced diagonally

4 bok choy, stems sliced and leaves
   left whole

2 zucchini, sliced diagonally

1-inch piece of ginger root, peeled
   and cut into thin strips

2 large garlic cloves, finely chopped

2 tablespoons Chinese cooking wine
   or dry sherry

1 teaspoon sesame oil

**1** Put the black beans in a bowl, cover with boiled water, and let soak 30 minutes. Drain, reserving 3 tablespoons of the soaking liquid. Mix together the soy sauce, cornstarch, and reserved soaking water and set aside.

**2** In a large wok, heat the sunflower oil to 350°F, or until a cube of bread turns golden in 40 seconds. Add half of the noodles—they should puff up, becoming light and crisp as soon as they are immersed in the oil. Using a slotted spoon, remove the noodles from the wok and drain on paper towels. Set aside while you cook the remaining noodles.

**3** Pour off all but 1 tablespoon of the oil from the wok and add the broccoli. Stir-fry over high heat 1 minute, then add the yellow pepper, scallions, bok choy, zucchini, ginger, garlic, and black beans and stir-fry 2 minutes longer.

**4** Reduce the heat to medium-low, add the Chinese wine, sesame oil, and soy sauce mixture and stir-fry briefly until slightly thicker. Divide the stir-fry into four shallow bowls, top with the crisp noodles, and serve immediately.

# SPICED SWEET POTATO, ZUCCHINI, AND RED PEPPER EGGAH

**SERVES 4**

12 ounces sweet potatoes, peeled
   and halved or quartered

2 tablespoons olive oil

1 tablespoon butter

1 onion, thinly sliced

1 zucchini, diced

2 garlic cloves, finely chopped

1 small red bell pepper, seeded and
   diced

a pinch of cayenne pepper

1 teaspoon cumin seeds

1 teaspoon coriander seeds, crushed

1 teaspoon dried thyme

6 eggs, lightly beaten

2 tablespoons chopped cilantro
   leaves

salt and freshly ground black pepper

**1** Boil the sweet potatoes 10 minutes, or until tender. Drain and let cool slightly, then cut into bite-size cubes.

**2** Preheat the broiler to high. Heat the oil and butter in a large, flameproof, nonstick skillet over medium-low heat. Fry the onion 8 minutes, reducing the heat to medium-low, or until soft, then add the zucchini, garlic, and red pepper and fry, stirring, 4 minutes longer. Stir in the cayenne, cumin and coriander seeds, and thyme and cook 1 minute. Stir in the sweet potatoes and spread the mixture out in an even layer in the pan.

**3** Season the beaten eggs with salt and pepper, add the cilantro leaves and pour the mixture over the vegetables. Cook over medium-low heat 3 minutes, or until the bottom is set and golden.

**4** To cook the top, put the pan under the broiler 2 minutes until set and light golden. Cut into wedges and serve.

# BRUSCHETTA WITH FETA, PUY LENTILS, AND ZUCCHINI RIBBONS

This is not a dainty bruschetta, normally served as a nibble with drinks, but one of substance that makes a filling meal served with a crisp green salad. It's best to use an open-textured bread for the bruschetta, and griddling the slices lends a characteristic smoky flavor.

**SERVES 4**

heaped ¾ cup Puy lentils
8 thick slices of ciabatta or pain de campagne
olive oil, for brushing
2 zucchini, thinly sliced lengthwise into thin ribbons
16 baby plum tomatoes, halved or quartered, if large
2 tablespoons chopped parsley leaves
6 ounces feta cheese, diced

**DRESSING**

1 red chili, seeded and finely chopped
1 tablespoon kecap manis
1 tablespoon balsamic vinegar
2 tablespoons extra-virgin olive oil, plus extra for drizzling (optional)
1 to 2 tablespoons lemon juice
1 garlic clove, crushed
salt and freshly ground black pepper

1 Put the lentils in a saucepan and cover with water. Bring to a boil, then reduce the heat to low, cover partially, and simmer 25 minutes, or until tender. Drain and transfer to a mixing bowl.

2 Meanwhile, heat a griddle pan over medium heat until hot and brush the slices of bread with olive oil. Griddle 3 or 4 slices at a time, depending on their size and arranging them diagonally in the pan, 5 to 7 minutes, turning once until toasted. Keep warm while you griddle the remaining slices, then set aside.

3 To griddle the zucchini, brush them with a little oil, then arrange them in the hot pan. Griddle 8 minutes, turning once, or until tender and charred in places.

4 When the lentils are cooked, mix together all of the ingredients for the dressing and pour it over the warm lentils. Add the tomatoes and parsley and toss well, then set aside.

5 Spoon the lentil mixture on top of the toasts and top with the feta and zucchini. Serve drizzled with extra olive oil, if desired.

# VIETNAMESE COCONUT CREPES WITH VEGETABLE STIR-FRY

Coconut milk adds a richness to these golden-colored savory crepes. They are slightly thicker than traditional French crepes and make a great base for the stir-fried vegetables in a sesame and ginger dressing featured here.

**SERVES 4**

1 tablespoon sunflower oil, plus extra for frying
½ cup cashew nuts
1 onion, sliced
6 ounces snow peas, trimmed
1 large carrot, thinly sliced diagonally
1 ¼ cups shredded Chinese leaves
1 garlic clove, crushed
1 tablespoon peeled and grated ginger root
sesame oil, for drizzling
2 tablespoons chopped cilantro leaves
2 tablespoons torn basil leaves
2 tablespoons chopped mint leaves

**COCONUT CREPES**

1 ¼ cups rice flour
½ teaspoon salt
1 teaspoon ground turmeric
1 large egg, lightly beaten
1 ¾ cups canned coconut milk

**SESAME AND GINGER DRESSING**

1 tablespoon rice wine vinegar
juice of 1 lime
2 tablespoons kecap manis
1 tablespoon sesame oil, plus extra for drizzling
1 tablespoon light brown sugar
1 tablespoon peeled and grated ginger root
1 small red chili, finely chopped
1 garlic clove, crushed
½ teaspoon salt

1 To make the crepes, sift the rice flour, salt and turmeric into a bowl. Slowly beat in the egg, coconut milk, and ¼ cup water to make a smooth, thin batter the consistency of light cream. Let stand 30 minutes.

2 Meanwhile, mix together all of the ingredients for the dressing in a small bowl and set aside.

3 Preheat the oven to 150°F. Heat a little oil in a large, nonstick skillet over medium heat and spread it over the bottom with a crumpled piece of paper towel. Add ½ cup of the batter to the pan and tilt to coat the bottom. Reduce the heat to medium-low and cook 1 ½ to 2 minutes on each side until light golden and set, then slide the crepe out of the pan on to a plate and keep warm. Repeat to make 3 more crepes, wiping the pan with extra oil, as necessary. (You might have a little batter left over; this allows for a couple of mishaps, as the first crepe doesn't always come out smoothly.) Cover the crepes with foil and keep warm in the oven while you cook the stir-fry.

4 Toast the cashews in a dry wok over medium heat for 2–3 minutes until light golden, then remove from the wok and set aside. Heat the sunflower oil in the wok over high heat and stir-fry the onion 3 minutes. Add the snow peas and carrot and stir-fry 2 minutes longer. Add the Chinese leaves, garlic, and ginger and stir-fry 1 minute longer, then drizzle with a little sesame oil.

5 Put 1 coconut crepe on each of four plates, top with the stir-fried vegetables, and spoon the dressing over the top. Sprinkle with the cashews, cilantro, basil, and mint and serve.

# RICE CAKES ON WILTED GREENS WITH LEMON–CHILI BUTTER

A Mediterranean twist on fried rice cakes, this recipe brings together the flavors of chilli, thyme, and feta in deliciously crisp bites.

**SERVES 4**

¾ cup brown basmati rice
5 scallions, finely chopped
1 carrot, cut into fine long strips
1 long red chili, seeded and finely
  chopped
1 tablespoon thyme leaves
2 eggs, lightly beaten
¼ cup all-purpose flour
¼ cup heavy cream
¾ cup crumbled feta cheese
¼ cup sunflower oil, for frying, plus
  extra as needed
salt and freshly ground black pepper

GREENS WITH LEMON–CHILI BUTTER

3 cups shredded greens, such as
  kale or savoy cabbage
1 red chili, seeded and thinly sliced
  into rounds
2 tablespoons butter
1 to 2 tablespoons lemon juice, plus
  lemon wedges, to serve

1 Put the rice in a saucepan and cover with cold water by about ½ inch. Bring to a boil, then reduce the heat to the lowest setting and simmer, covered, 25 to 30 minutes until tender and the water is absorbed. Remove the pan from the heat and set aside, covered, 5 minutes. Spread the rice out on a baking sheet and let cool completely.

2 Transfer the rice to a large bowl and mix in the scallions, carrot, chili, thyme, eggs, flour, and cream. Season with salt and pepper and stir until combined. Gently stir in the feta, taking care not to break it up too much.

3 Preheat the oven to 150°F. Heat the sunflower oil in a large, nonstick skillet over medium heat. For each fritter, pile one-quarter of the mixture in a mound in the pan, then flatten slightly with a spatula—they should be about ¾ inch thick. Reduce the heat to medium-low and cook 2 cakes at a time 3 minutes on each side, then drain on paper towels. Transfer to an ovenproof plate, cover with foil, and keep warm in the oven while you make the remaining 2 fritters. Add more oil to the pan, if needed.

4 Meanwhile, blanch the spring greens in boiling water 2 minutes, then drain and return to the pan. Add the chili and butter and toss until coated. Season with salt and pepper and stir in the lemon juice.

5 Divide the cabbage onto four plates and drizzle with any buttery juices left in the pan. Top each portion with a rice cake and serve.

# GYOZA IN LEMONGRASS BROTH WITH CHAR-BROILED ASPARAGUS

Gyoza, also known as potstickers, are popular dumplings in Japan. Gyoza wrappers are slightly thicker than wonton wrappers (which you can also use here). You can also steam or pan-fry the gyoza.

**SERVES 4**

16 asparagus spears, trimmed
2 teaspoons sesame oil
2 teaspoons sunflower oil
3 tablespoons chopped cilantro leaves

GYOZA

2 cups cooked adzuki beans
1 teaspoon sesame oil
2 tablespoons light soy sauce
3 tablespoons coarsely grated unpeeled ginger root
3 scallions, finely chopped
2 garlic cloves, crushed
½ teaspoon cornstarch
⅔ cup finely chopped white cabbage
24 gyoza wrappers, defrosted
1¾ cups sunflower oil, for deep-frying
salt and freshly ground black pepper

LEMONGRASS BROTH

5 cups vegetable stock
2 lemongrass sticks, crushed with outer leaves removed
4 kaffir lime leaves
2 ounces ginger root, peeled and thinly sliced crosswise
1 tablespoon vegetarian fish sauce
juice of 1 lime
½ teaspoon granulated sugar
1¼ cups canned coconut milk
1 long red chili, seeded and sliced

1 First make the gyoza. Put the adzuki beans, sesame oil, and half the soy sauce in a bowl and mash lightly with the back of a fork, leaving some of the beans whole. Stir in the ginger, scallions, garlic, cornstarch, and cabbage. Season with salt and pepper to taste and mix well.

2 Put 1 heaped tablespoon of the filling in the middle of a gyoza wrapper—you want the gyozas to be as full as possible. Brush the edge of the wrapper with water, top with another wrapper, and press the edges to seal. Set aside and repeat to make 11 more gyoza.

3 To make the lemongrass broth, put the stock, lemongrass, lime leaves, ginger, vegetarian fish sauce, lime juice, and sugar in a large saucepan. Bring to a boil, then reduce the heat to low, and simmer 15 minutes. Strain the stock into a clean bowl, discarding the solids, and return to the saucepan. Add the remaining soy sauce, coconut milk, and chili and cook 5 minutes longer, or until slightly reduced and thickened. Season with salt and pepper.

4 Meanwhile, preheat the oven to 150°F and heat a griddle pan over medium heat. Toss the asparagus in the sesame and sunflower oils and griddle 5 to 7 minutes, turning occasionally, until tender and charred in places. Transfer to an ovenproof plate and keep warm in the oven.

5 To deep-fry the gyoza, heat the remaining sunflower oil in a deep saucepan to 350°F, or until a cube of bread turns golden in 40 seconds. Fry the gyoza, 3 at a time, 2 minutes, turning once, until golden and puffed up. Remove, using a slotted spoon, and drain on paper towels. Transfer to an ovenproof plate and keep warm in the oven while you cook the remaining gyoza.

6 To serve, reheat the lemongrass broth, if necessary, then ladle it into four large, shallow bowls. Sprinkle with the cilantro and put 3 gyoza in the middle of each bowl, slightly overlapping them. Arrange the asparagus on top and serve immediately.

# BATTERED TOFU WITH CRUSHED MINT EDAMAME AND SWEET POTATO FRIES

A twist on the classic British fish and chips. Make sure the oil is heated to the correct temperature when frying the tofu to guarantee a crisp, golden batter—the same goes for the sweet potato fries, as there's nothing worse than soggy fries.

**SERVES 4**

¾ cup all-purpose flour, plus extra for dusting

½ teaspoon salt, plus extra to serve

½ teaspoon cayenne pepper

1 egg, lightly beaten

7 tablespoons light ale or beer

14 ounces firm tofu, patted dry and cut into 12 x ½-inch thick slices

2 cups sunflower oil, for deep-frying

1 pound 12 ounces sweet potatoes, peeled, trimmed, and cut into thick fries

freshly ground black pepper

**MINT EDAMAME**

1⅔ cups frozen shelled edamame (soy) beans

3 tablespoons butter

1 tablespoon peeled and finely grated ginger root

1 handful of chopped mint leaves

1 red chili, seeded and finely chopped

1 To make the batter, sift the flour, salt, and cayenne into a mixing bowl. Gradually, stir in the egg and ale to make a smooth batter, then set aside to rest 20 minutes.

2 Preheat the oven to 150°F. To deep-fry the tofu, heat the sunflower oil in a wide, deep saucepan to 350°F, or until a cube of bread turns golden in 40 seconds. Dust each slice of tofu in flour, dip it in the batter, and carefully lower it into the hot oil. Deep-fry 4 slices at a time 3 to 4 minutes until golden and crisp, then drain on paper towels. Transfer to an ovenproof plate and keep warm in the oven while you repeat with the remaining tofu and batter.

3 To deep-fry the sweet potato fries, reheat the oil if necessary. Add half of the sweet potatoes and fry 5 minutes, or until crisp and golden, then drain on paper towels. Transfer to an ovenproof plate and keep warm in the oven while you repeat with the remaining sweet potatoes.

4 Meanwhile, boil the edamame beans 3 to 5 minutes until tender. Drain, return to the pan, and add the butter, ginger, mint, and chili. Heat over medium-low heat, stirring, until the beans are coated, then lightly crush with the back of a fork.

5 Pile the sweet potatoes onto four plates and season with salt and pepper. Top with the tofu and serve immediately with the edamame beans.

# UDON NOODLES WITH SNOW PEAS IN SICHUAN DRESSING

The spicy, peanutty dressing in this recipe is a perfect complement to the soft and satisfying stir-fried noodles and crisp snow peas and peppers.

**SERVES 4**
5 scallions
1 tablespoon peanut oil
1 large red bell pepper, seeded and
    sliced into long strips
6 ounces snow peas
1 ¾ cooked udon noodles
1 handful of bean sprouts
a few cilantro leaves
3 tablespoons sunflower seeds,
    toasted
heaped 2 tablespoons broccoli
    sprouts

**SICHUAN DRESSING**
6 tablespoons smooth peanut butter
⅔ cup vegetable stock
2 tablespoons light soy sauce
2 teaspoons sesame oil
1 tablespoon peanut oil
3 garlic cloves, crushed
2-inch piece of ginger root, peeled
    and grated
2 red chilies, seeded and chopped

1 To make the Sichuan dressing, mix together the peanut butter, stock, soy sauce, sesame oil, and 5 tablespoons water. Heat a large wok over medium heat, add the peanut oil, and stir-fry the garlic, ginger, and chilies 1 minute. Remove the wok from the heat and stir in the peanut butter mixture, then transfer to a bowl and set aside.

2 Thinly slice 3 of the scallions diagonally and cut the remaining scallions into thin, long strips. Wipe the wok clean and heat it over high heat. Add the peanut oil and stir-fry the sliced scallions, red pepper, and snow peas 2 minutes. Remove from the wok, using a slotted spoon, and set aside.

3 Add the udon noodles and dressing to the wok and stir gently to separate and coat the noodles in the dressing. Add the stir-fried vegetables and bean sprouts and cook, stirring, 3 minutes until warmed through.

4 Divide the udon noodles and broth into four large bowls. Sprinkle with the scallion strips, cilantro, sunflower seeds, and broccoli sprouts and serve immediately.

# WARM ZUCCHINI, MARJORAM, AND LEMON SALAD

**SERVES 4**

3 tablespoons extra-virgin olive oil

2 garlic cloves, thinly sliced

3 zucchini, sliced diagonally

2 tablespoons marjoram or oregano
leaves

2 tablespoons lemon juice

salt and freshly ground black pepper

1 Heat the olive oil in a large, nonstick skillet over medium heat. Add the garlic and zucchini and sauté, stirring regularly, 3 minutes, or until soft.

2 Reduce the heat to low, stir in the marjoram and lemon juice, and season with salt and black pepper, then serve.

# SESAME AND TAHINI SPINACH

**SERVES 4**

1 tablespoon sesame seeds

1 tablespoon sunflower oil

2 garlic cloves, finely chopped

14 ounces spinach leaves, tough
stems removed

2 tablespoons mirin or dry sherry

1 tablespoon light tahini

2 teaspoons toasted sesame oil

salt and freshly ground black pepper

1 Toast the sesame seeds in a dry wok over low heat 5 to 7 minutes, stirring occasionally, until golden, then transfer to a bowl.

2 Heat the sunflower oil in the wok over medium-low heat and fry the garlic 30 seconds. Add the spinach and stir-fry 2 minutes until it wilts.

3 Add the mirin, tahini, sesame oil, and 2 tablespoons water and toss until the spinach is coated. Season with salt and pepper to taste, sprinkle with the sesame seeds, and serve.

# SLOW-COOKED POTATOES

Cooking the potatoes slowly over very low heat makes them meltingly soft and tender, with a crust that's golden and slightly sticky — pure comfort food!

**SERVES 4**

5 saffron strands

7 tablespoons hot vegetable stock

2 tablespoons butter

3 tablespoons olive oil

1 pound 8 ounces potatoes, peeled
and thinly sliced

4 garlic cloves, sliced

salt and freshly ground black pepper

1 Stir the saffron into the stock and let infuse 5 minutes. Meanwhile, heat the butter and oil in a large, deep, nonstick skillet over medium-high heat and sauté the potatoes 3 to 4 minutes until just starting to color, working in batches if necessary, to avoid overcrowding the pan.

2 Arrange the potatoes in two even layers in the pan, reduce the heat to medium-low, and pour the saffron stock over them. Sprinkle the garlic over the top and season with salt and pepper.

3 Bring to a boil, then reduce the heat to low. Cover snugly with a circle of baking parchment paper to prevent the potatoes from drying out. Cover with a tight-fitting lid and cook, without stirring, 40 minutes or until the potatoes are very tender, then serve.

# CAULIFLOWER AND POTATO WITH CRISP CURRY LEAVES

Potatoes, cauliflower, and spices are natural partners. In this recipe, the cumin and mustard seeds, and the curry leaves complement the flavor of the cauliflower especially well.

**SERVES 4**

2 potatoes, peeled and halved
2 cups cauliflower florets
2 tablespoons sunflower oil
2 curry leaf sprigs
2 large garlic cloves, thinly sliced
2 teaspoons cumin seeds
2 teaspoons yellow mustard seeds
2 teaspoons fennel seeds
1 red chili, seeded and finely chopped
1 teaspoon turmeric
2 tablespoons lemon juice
salt and freshly ground black pepper

1 Steam the potatoes 12 minutes or until tender. Remove from the steamer and set aside to cool slightly, then cut into bite-size cubes. Steam the cauliflower 3 minutes until just tender, then refresh under cold running water and set aside.

2 Heat the sunflower oil in a large wok over medium heat and fry the curry leaves 2 to 3 minutes until crisp. Remove from the pan, using a slotted spoon, drain on paper towels, and set aside. Add the garlic, cumin, mustard and fennel seeds, and chili to the pan and fry, stirring, 1 minute.

3 Add the potatoes and cauliflower and turn to coat in the spice mixture. Stir in the turmeric and lemon juice, then season with salt and pepper. Top with the curry leaves and serve.

# GINGER-GLAZED BRUSSELS SPROUTS AND SHALLOTS

The poor sprout has a tainted image, but when stir-fried briefly it retains its vibrant color and crisp texture and is milder in flavor.

**SERVES 4**

7 ounces small shallots, peeled
7 ounces Brussels sprouts, peeled and trimmed
2 tablespoons sunflower oil
2 tablespoons butter
2-inch piece of ginger root, peeled and finely chopped
4 teaspoons honey
salt and freshly ground black pepper

1 Blanch the shallots in boiling water 2 minutes, then add the sprouts and cook 2 minutes longer. Drain and refresh under cold running water.

2 Heat the sunflower oil in a wok over medium heat, add the shallots and sprouts, and stir-fry 3 minutes, or until soft. Reduce the heat slightly and add the butter. When it melts stir in the ginger and honey and season to taste with salt and pepper.

3 Stir-fry 1 minute longer, or until the vegetables are coated in a glossy honey glaze, then serve.

# SWEET VANILLA RISOTTO CAKES WITH CARAMEL DRIZZLE

The same rules apply when making a sweet risotto as a savory one—gradually stir in the liquid, in this case, the vanilla-infused milk, until the rice grains are creamy and tender.

**SERVES 4**

4 cups whole milk

1 vanilla bean, split lengthwise and seeds scraped out, or 2 teaspoons vanilla bean paste

2 tablespoons butter, plus extra for frying

1 cup arborio rice

¼ cup raisins (optional)

¼ cup granulated sugar

**CARAMEL DRIZZLE**

½ cup granulated sugar

2 tablespoons butter

6 tablespoons heavy cream

1 Bring the milk and vanilla bean and seeds to just below a boil in a saucepan over medium-low heat, then remove the pan from the heat and let stand 5 minutes to let the vanilla infuse the milk.

2 Melt the butter in a heavy-bottomed saucepan over medium-low heat, add the rice, and stir 2 minutes, or until the rice is coated in the butter and glossy. Remove the vanilla bean from the milk and discard. Stir in the raisins, if using, then add the milk a little at a time. Cook, stirring continuously, 25 minutes, or until all of the milk is absorbed and the rice is soft and creamy. Stir in the sugar and remove from the heat, then set aside to cool 5 minutes.

3 Line a square 7-inch baking pan or dish with baking parchment paper. Transfer the risotto to the dish, spreading it out in an even layer about ¾ inch thick. Smooth the top with a wet metal spatula, then let cool completely and set.

4 Turn the rice out of the pan and cut into 9 squares, using a wet metal spatula or knife, then set aside.

5 To make the caramel drizzle, put the sugar and 3 tablespoons water in a deep-sided saucepan. Heat over low heat 3 to 5 minutes, stirring continuously, until it comes to a boil and the sugar dissolves. Continue to cook until the sugar turns a deep golden color, swirling the pan occasionally rather than stirring at this stage. Remove from the heat and stir in the butter, then add the cream, taking care as it might froth up and splutter—it's a good idea to wear an oven glove. Reheat over low heat, beating until smooth and creamy, then set aside.

6 Preheat the oven to 150°F. Over medium heat, melt enough butter to coat the bottom of a large nonstick skillet. Fry half of the risotto cakes 3 minutes on each side, or until golden, reducing the heat to medium-low if necessary. Transfer the cakes to an ovenproof plate and keep warm in the oven while you cook the remaining cakes.

7 Put 2 risotto cakes on each of four plates (there will be 1 left over). Drizzle with the caramel sauce and serve.

# RUM BANANAS WITH COCONUT—LIME CREAM AND WONTON CHIPS

**SERVES 4**

3 tablespoons butter

4 large, just-ripe bananas

2 tablespoons honey

1 teaspoon pumpkin pie spice

¼ cup dark rum

**COCONUT AND LIME CREAM**

6 tablespoons whole-milk plain yogurt

heaped 2 tablespoons coconut cream

1 tablespoon confectioners' sugar

finely grated zest of ½ lime

**WONTON CHIPS**

½ cup sunflower oil, for frying

4 square wonton wrappers

2 tablespoons honey

1 tablespoon sesame seeds

1 To make the wonton chips, heat the sunflower oil in a skillet to 325°F, or until a piece of bread dropped in browns in 50 seconds. Working in batches, fry the wonton wrappers 1 minute on each side, or until golden and crisp, then drain on paper towels. Heat the honey in a small saucepan and brush it over 1 side of each chips. Sprinkle with the sesame seeds and set aside.

2 To make the coconut and lime cream, mix together the yogurt, coconut cream, and confections' sugar in a small bowl. Sprinkle the lime zest over the top and set aside.

3 Melt the butter in a large, nonstick skillet over medium-low heat. Peel the bananas and cut them in half lengthwise, then put them in a single layer in the pan, working in batches, if necessary. Cook 1 minute on each side, then carefully remove them from the pan.

4 Add the honey, mixed spice, and rum to the pan and cook 1 minute, stirring, or until the sauce starts to thicken. Return the bananas to the pan and spoon the sauce over them to coat. Cook 2 minutes loner, or until the fruit is tender and the sauce is syrupy. Serve the bananas topped with the sauce, accompanied by the coconut—lime cream and wonton chips.

# ALLSPICE FRENCH TOAST WITH LEMONGRASS NECTARINES

**SERVES 4**

2 eggs, lightly beaten

¼ cup milk

1 teaspoon vanilla extract

1 teaspoon ground allspice

1 tablespoon maple syrup, plus extra for drizzling

3 tablespoons butter

4 thick slices of brioche

Greek yogurt, to serve

**LEMONGRASS NECTARINES**

1 large lemongrass stick, crushed with outer leaves removed

1 tablespoon granulated sugar

3 slightly underripe nectarines, halved, pitted, and thickly sliced

1 Preheat the oven to 150°F. To prepare the nectarines, put the lemongrass, sugar, and ½ cup water in a saucepan and bring to a boil, stirring. Reduce the heat to low, add the nectarines and simmer 5 to 7 minutes until tender. Remove the pan from the heat and let the nectarines steep in the flavored syrup. Taste and add more sugar, if necessary.

2 In a shallow dish, beat together the eggs, milk, vanilla extract, allspice, and maple syrup.

3 Melt half of the butter in a large, nonstick skillet over medium heat. Dunk both sides of 2 of the brioche slices into the egg mixture, then cook them 3 to 4 minutes, turning once, until golden. Transfer to a plate and keep warm while you repeat with the remaining brioche.

4 Divide the French toast onto four plates and drizzle with a little extra maple syrup, if desired. Remove the lemongrass from the nectarine, then spoon the nectarines and a little of the lemongrass syrup alongside. Serve immediately with yogurt.

# BUTTERMILK AND SOUR CHERRY PANCAKES

**SERVES 4**

scant 1 ½ cups all-purpose flour
a large pinch of salt
1 teaspoon cinnamon
1 teaspoon baking soda
3 tablespoons granulated sugar
2 large eggs, lightly beaten
1 ¼ cups buttermilk
3 tablespoons milk
1 cup dried sour cherries
sunflower oil, for frying
blueberries, to serve
Greek yogurt, to serve
maple syrup, for drizzling

1 Sift the flour, salt, cinnamon, baking soda, and sugar into a large mixing bowl. Stir until combined, then make a well in the middle. Add the eggs, buttermilk, and milk to the well and gradually work in the dry ingredients, beating to make a smooth, thick batter. Let rest 20 minutes, then stir in the dried cherries.

2 Preheat the oven to 150°F. Heat a little oil over medium heat in a large, nonstick skillet, and wipe away any excess with a crumpled piece of paper towel. Drop 3 spoonfuls of the batter into the pan, spacing them apart. Reduce the heat to medium-low and cook 2 to 3 minutes until bubbles appear on the surface, then flip over and cook 2 minutes longer. Transfer to an ovenproof plate and keep warm in the oven while you cook the remaining pancakes.

3 Serve 3 pancakes per person. Top with blueberries and a generous spoonful of yogurt, then drizzle with maple syrup and serve.

# BANANA AND APPLE SESAME FRITTERS

**SERVES 4**

⅔ cup all-purpose flour
a large pinch of salt
5 tablespoons milk
2 cups sunflower oil
2 large egg whites
2 tablespoons sesame seeds
3 bananas
2 apples
1 tablespoon lemon juice
sugar, for dusting

1 Sift the flour and salt into a mixing bowl. Make a well in the middle, add the milk, 1 tablespoon of the sunflower oil, and 5 tablespoons water to the well and gradually work in the flour, beating to make a thick, smooth batter. Let the batter rest 20 minutes.

2 Preheat the oven to 150°F. Beat the egg whites in a separate clean bowl until they form soft peaks, then fold them into the batter in 2 batches. Stir in the sesame seeds.

3 Peel the bananas, halve them crosswise. and then cut in half again lengthwise. Peel the apples (there is no need to core them), then cut into ¼-inch slices, discarding any seeds. Brush bananas and apples with lemon juice to prevent them browning.

4 To deep-fry the fritters, heat the remaining oil in a wide, deep saucepan to 350°F, or until a piece of bread turns golden in 40 seconds. Dunk the banana slices into the batter, one at a time, and fry 5 pieces at a time 2 to 3 minutes until golden. Using a slotted spoon, remove the fritters and drain on paper towels. Transfer to an ovenproof plate and keep warm in the oven while you fry the remaining banana fritters. Pat the apple slices dry with paper towels and fry in the same way. When all the fritters are cooked, sprinkle them with sugar and serve immediately.

# CINNAMON-DUSTED DOUGHNUTS WITH CHOCOLATE SAUCE

These light and fluffy doughnuts are infused with orange zest and are best eaten warm, soon after cooking—perfect dunked into the rich chocolate sauce.

**SERVES 4 TO 6**

7 tablespoons light cream

1 extra-large egg, lightly beaten

5 tablespoons granulated sugar

7 tablespoons freshly squeezed orange juice

finely grated zest of 1 orange

3 tablespoons olive oil

3 cups self-rising flour, plus extra for kneading

2 cups sunflower oil, for deep frying

**CINNAMON DUST**

5 tablespoons granulated sugar

1 teaspoon cinnamon

**CHOCOLATE SAUCE**

1 cup less 2 tablespoons milk

1 3/4 ounces dark chocolate, broken into small chunks

2 teaspoons cornstarch

scant 1/4 cup granulated sugar

1 In a large mixing bowl, beat the cream, egg, sugar, orange juice, orange zest, and olive oil until combined. Sift in the flour and mix to make a soft dough.

2 Turn out the dough and knead it on a lightly floured work surface 1 minute to form a soft ball of dough. Using floured hands, divide the dough into 16 equal pieces. Roll out each piece with your hands into a rope shape, about 6 inches long, then press the ends together to form a ring. Run your finger around the inside to make a hole, then transfer to a lightly floured plate.

3 To make the cinnamon dust, mix together the granulated sugar and cinnamon on a plate and set aside. To make the chocolate sauce, put half of the milk in a saucepan over medium heat and bring to just below the boil. Reduce the heat to low, add the chocolate, and stir until melted. Mix together the remaining milk, cornstarch, and sugar in a bowl and add it to the chocolate milk mixture. Stir over medium-low heat 3 to 5 minutes until thick, then transfer to a serving bowl.

4 Preheat the oven to 150°F, and heat the sunflower oil in a wide, deep saucepan to 350°F, or until a piece of bread turns golden after 40 seconds. Fry the doughnuts, 3 at a time, about 4 minutes, turning once, until golden. Remove with a slotted spoon and drain on paper towels, then transfer to an ovenproof plate and keep warm in the oven while you fry the remaining doughnuts.

5 Roll the doughnuts in the cinnamon dust until lightly coated. Serve warm with the chocolate sauce.

Gentle and healthy, steaming is perfect for cooking delicate ingredients and retaining precious nutrients. Surprisingly versatile, it's ideal for cooking vegetables quickly to create clean, fresh flavors and keep their crisp texture, as well as slow-cooking dishes, such as the ultimate comfort food—puddings.

# STEAM

Crushed Pea and Ginger Wontons, page 129

# SPRING VEGETABLES WITH CRUNCHY WALNUT CRUMBLE

I love the contrast in texture and color in this dish, from the crunchy, garlicky, nutty crumbs to the steamed delicate freshness of the spring vegetables.

**SERVES 4**

⅔ cup shelled fava beans

7 ounces baby carrots, trimmed

5 ounces thin green beans

5 ounces asparagus, trimmed

5 ounces baby zucchini, halved lengthwise

1 tablespoon olive oil

1 tablespoon lemon juice

½ teaspoon Dijon mustard

sea salt and freshly ground black pepper

**WALNUT CRUST**

⅔ cup walnut halves

1 tablespoon olive oil

2 tablespoons butter

1¼ cups fresh white bread crumbs

1 large garlic clove, finely chopped

1 red chili, seeded and chopped

**HARISSA MAYONNAISE**

½ cup mayonnaise

1 garlic clove, finely minced

1 teaspoon harissa paste

**1** Meanwhile, mix together the mayonnaise, garlic, and harissa and serve with the vegetables.

**2** To make the walnut crumble, toast the walnuts in a dry skillet over medium heat 4 to 5 minutes, turning occasionally, until light golden, then chop coarsely and set aside. Heat the olive oil and butter in a skillet over medium-high heat and fry the bread crumbs 3 minutes, stirring often, or until they are crisp and light golden. Add the garlic and chili, then cook, stirring, 2 minutes longer. Remove from the heat and stir in the walnuts.

**3** Steam the fava beans 3 minutes, then, when cool enough to handle, pop them out of their outer shells to reveal the bright green beans inside. Keep them warm while you steam the carrots and green beans 5 minutes or until tender. Again, keep the vegetables warm while you steam the asparagus and zucchini 3 minutes or until tender.

**4** Meanwhile, mix together the olive oil, lemon juice, and mustard and season with salt and pepper. Pour this dressing over the warm vegetables, sprinkle the walnut crust over the top, and serve with the harissa mayonnaise.

# WARM BROCCOLI, MOZZARELLA, AND CHILI SALAD

**SERVES 4**

14 ounces long-stem broccoli, trimmed

¼ cup olive oil

2 large garlic cloves, thinly sliced

1 long red chili, seeded and thinly sliced

2 tablespoons small capers, rinsed and drained

¼ cup lemon juice

9 ounces mozzarella cheese, preferably buffalo, drained

salt and freshly ground black pepper

a few basil leaves, to serve

1 Steam the broccoli 3 to 4 minutes until tender.

2 Meanwhile, heat the oil in a saucepan over medium-low heat and fry the garlic, chili, and capers 1 minute, stirring often. Add the lemon juice and season with salt and pepper.

3 Put the warm broccoli on a serving plate. Tear the mozzarella into chunks and sprinkle it over the top. Pour the garlic mixture over the broccoli and mozzarella, sprinkle with the basil leaves, and serve.

# JAPANESE SOBA NOODLE SALAD WITH SESAME–TOFU DRESSING

You can make the noodles and vegetables ahead of time, simply refresh them under cold running water and store in airtight containers until ready to use.

**SERVES 4**

9 ounces soba noodles

2 tablespoons sesame seeds

2 carrots, sliced into thin ribbons

2 leeks, halved crosswise and sliced lengthwise into thin strips

1 cup snow peas

7 ounces asparagus tips, trimmed

2 tablespoons finely chopped chives

½ teaspoon togarashi seasoning (optional)

SESAME–TOFU DRESSING

3 ounces silken tofu

1 tablespoon tamari soy sauce

2 tablespoons mirin

2 teaspoons peeled and finely grated ginger root

1 teaspoon granulated sugar

salt and freshly ground black pepper

1 Cook the noodles in plenty of boiling salted water following the package directions, then drain.

2 Meanwhile, toast the sesame seeds in a dry skillet over medium-low heat 3 to 5 minutes, shaking the pan occasionally, until light golden, then set aside. Steam the carrots, leeks, snow peas, and asparagus 3 minutes, or until tender.

3 To make the dressing, blend together the tofu, tamari, mirin, ginger, and sugar, adding 1 tablespoon of the toasted sesame seeds, and season with salt and pepper.

4 Toss the noodles with half of the dressing, then divide onto four plates. Top with the vegetables and drizzle with the remaining dressing. Sprinkle with the remaining sesame seeds, chives, and togarashi seasoning and serve warm or at room temperature.

# CHINESE RICE IN BEANCURD POCKETS

Abura-age is a Japanese deep-fried tofu (beancurd) bundle available from oriental grocery stores. Normally sold frozen, they defrost in minutes and can then be split open and stuffed. Here, they are filled with a mixture of vegetables and herbs and served with a chili and hoisin dipping sauce.

**SERVES 4**

½ ounce dried shiitake mushrooms

1 large carrot, grated

4 scallions, thinly sliced

2 cups shredded Chinese cabbage

2 garlic cloves, crushed

4 water chestnuts, finely chopped

2 tablespoons chopped cilantro leaves, plus extra to serve

1 tablespoon light soy sauce

1 tablespoon peeled and finely grated ginger root

6 deep-fried tofu bundles (abura-age), defrosted if frozen

**DIPPING SAUCE**

¼ cup sweet chili sauce

2 tablespoons light soy sauce

2 tablespoons hoisin sauce

2 tablespoons crushed unsalted peanuts

1 Soak the shiitake mushrooms in hot water 20 minutes, or until soft. Drain them well, squeeze out any excess water, and finely chop, then set aside.

2 Meanwhile, make the dipping sauce. In a small bowl, mix together all of the ingredients for the sauce and 1 tablespoon water, then set aside.

3 In another bowl, mix together the shiitake mushrooms, carrot, scallions, Chinese leaves, garlic, water chestnuts, cilantro leaves, soy sauce, and ginger.

4 Cut the tofu bundles in half crosswise and open each one out to make a pocket. Stuff with the vegetable mixture and stand the pockets upright in a steamer lined with baking parchment paper. (Use a tiered steamer if you have one or steam the pockets in two batches, keeping them warm as needed.) Cover and steam 6 to 8 minutes until the vegetables are tender.

5 Sprinkle the stuffed beancurd pockets with extra cilantro and serve with the dipping sauce on the side, allowing 3 bundles per person.

# CRUSHED PEA AND GINGER WONTONS

Vibrant in color and packed with oriental flavors, these pea dumplings make a perfect light lunch accompanied by miso soup, or an elegant appetizer. Choose wonton wrappers specifically for steaming, and if you don't have a bamboo steamer, use a regular metal one.

**MAKES 32 (SERVES 4 TO 6)**

1²/₃ cups frozen peas

3 scallions, finely chopped

1½-inch piece of ginger root, peeled and very finely chopped

1 teaspoon soy sauce, plus extra to serve

32 wonton wrappers, defrosted if frozen

1 small red chili, seeded and finely sliced (optional)

a few chives, finely chopped, to serve

freshly ground black pepper

1 Steam the peas 3 minutes or until tender, then drain, if necessary, and transfer to a mixing bowl. Mash with a potato masher or the back of a fork until crushed but not completely smooth. Stir in the scallions, ginger, and soy sauce, then season with pepper.

2 Put 1 wonton wrapper on a plate, keeping the others covered with a clean damp dish towel. Put 1 heaped teaspoon of the pea mixture in the middle and brush the edges of the wrapper with water. Gather up the sides around the filling and pinch together at the top to seal—it should look similar to a moneybag. Set the dumpling aside, covered with another clean damp dish towel, and repeat with the remaining wonton wrappers and filling.

3 Put 8 of the dumplings in a large bamboo steamer lined with baking parchment paper. Cover and steam over a wok of simmering water 8 minutes until the wonton wrappers are cooked and slightly translucent. Transfer the cooked dumplings to a plate and cover to keep warm while you steam the remaining dumplings. If necessary, occasionally replenish the water in the wok to prevent it from drying out during steaming.

4 To serve, pour a little soy sauce in four or six small dishes (one per person), then divide the chili, if using, among them. Sprinkle the dumplings with chives and serve warm with the dipping sauce.

# SUSHI BOWL WITH WASABI CASHEWS

**SERVES 4**

1½ cups sushi rice

2 tablespoons ume plum seasoning
    or rice vinegar

¼ cup freshly squeezed orange
    juice

1 tablespoon sesame oil, plus extra
    for dressing the vegetables

2 tablespoons light soy sauce, plus
    extra for dressing the vegetables

²⁄₃ cup trimmed and diagonally
    sliced green beans

¾ cup shelled edamame beans

1 large carrot, cut into fine strips

4 teaspoons sesame seeds, toasted

¼ nori sheet, cut into fine strips

¾ ounce pink pickled ginger,
    to serve

**JAPANESE OMELET**

2 extra-large eggs, plus 1 extra-large
    egg yolk

1 teaspoon light soy sauce

1 teaspoon granulated sugar

sunflower oil, for frying

**WASABI CASHEWS**

½ cup cashew nuts

1 tablespoon granulated sugar

heaped 1 tablespoon wasabi paste

a generous pinch of salt

1 Preheat the oven to 225°F. To make the wasabi cashews, toast the cashews in a dry skillet over medium heat 5 minutes, turning occasionally, until light golden, then set aside. Put the sugar and 1 tablespoon water in a small pan and bring to a boil, then reduce the heat and stir until the sugar dissolves. Remove the pan from the heat and stir in the wasabi and salt, then add the cashews. Stir until the cashews are coated in the wasabi mixture. Transfer to a baking tray lined with baking parchment paper and roast 35 to 40 minutes until crunchy, then set aside. They might still be a little sticky when they some out of the oven, but they will dry when cooled.

2 Wash the rice in several changes of water, then drain and transfer to a heavy-bottomed saucepan. Add enough water to cover the rice by ½ inch and bring to a boil. Reduce the heat to low, stir, cover with a tight-fitting lid, and simmer 10 to 12 minutes until the water is absorbed. Remove the pan from the heat and let stand, covered, 10 minutes. Meanwhile, mix together the ume plum seasoning, orange juice, sesame oil, and soy sauce to make a dressing for the rice.

3 Transfer the hot rice to a bowl and carefully fold in the dressing—do not stir. Cover with a plate and set aside.

4 To make the Japanese omelet, lightly whisk together the eggs, the extra yolk, soy sauce, sugar, and 2 tablespoons water in a bowl. Heat a large, nonstick skillet over medium-low heat, add a little sunflower oil, and wipe away any excess using paper towels. Add the egg mixture and swirl it around the pan. Cook 3 to 5 minutes or until half set. Fold it in half, then fold in the 2 sides to make a package. Turn the omelet over and cook briefly, then slide it out of the pan and cut into thin strips.

5 Meanwhile, steam the green beans 2 minutes. Add the edamames and carrots and steam 2 to 3 minutes longer until all the vegetables are tender. Transfer to a bowl and toss with a little sesame oil and soy sauce to taste. Sprinkle with the sesame seeds.

6 To serve, spoon one-quarter of the rice into a small bowl and press down to level the top, then turn it out onto a serving plate. Repeat with the remaining rice. Top each portion of rice with the nori, egg, and wasabi cashews and serve with the vegetables and pickled ginger alongside. You can also present this dish in a more relaxed way, with the vegetables and omelet mixed casually into the rice.

# CREAMY LEEK AND CHEESE ROULADES

Similar in texture to traditional British suet pastry, these creamy leek and cheese-filled roulades make a substantial weekend lunch.

**SERVES 4**

heaped 2 cups self-rising flour, plus extra for kneading

2 teaspoons baking powder

1 teaspoon vegetable bouillon powder

1 teaspoon English mustard powder

a generous pinch of salt, plus extra to season

6 tablespoons butter

2 tablespoons finely chopped chives

1 extra-large egg, lightly beaten

$\frac{1}{3}$ to scant $\frac{1}{2}$ cup milk

freshly ground black pepper

1 recipe quantity Watercress Sauce (see page 67)

**FILLING**

1 tablespoon olive oil

1 onion, finely chopped

2 leeks, finely chopped

1 tablespoon thyme leaves

2 tablespoons crème fraîche or sour cream

2 teaspoons Dijon mustard

$\frac{3}{4}$ cup grated sharp cheddar cheese

1 Sift the flour, baking powder, bouillon, mustard powder, and salt into a mixing bowl. Rub in the butter until the mixture resembles coarse crumbs, then stir in the chives, egg, and $\frac{1}{3}$ cup of the milk. Bring the dough together with your hands and knead lightly on a lightly floured surface to make a soft ball of dough, adding a little extra milk if it's too dry. Set aside, wrapped in plastic wrap, while you prepare the filling.

2 Heat the olive oil in a skillet over medium-low heat. Add the onion and leeks, cover, and cook 5 minutes, stirring occasionally, until soft. Remove the pan from the heat and stir in the thyme, crème fraîche, mustard, and cheese. Season with salt and pepper.

3 Divide the dough into 4 equal pieces. On a lightly floured surface, roll each one out into a rectangle about 5½ x 5 inches. Spoon one-quarter of the leek mixture down the middle of each rectangle and roll into a large log, enclosing the filling. Wet the edge and ends then press gently to seal. Prick the top 3 times and roll each roulade in baking parchment paper, twisting the ends of the paper closed.

4 Put the roulades in a large steamer, cover, and steam 18 to 20 minutes until risen and cooked through—they will look like long dumplings. Unwrap and slice each roulade in half diagonally. Serve with the watercress sauce.

# THAI TOFU AND VEGETABLES IN BANANA LEAVES

Banana leaves make attractive packages and are available at Asian grocery stores, but if you can't find them, you can use baking parchment paper instead. Serve these packages with Thai jasmine rice.

**SERVES 4**

4 small banana leaves

2 blocks of firm tofu, each about 9 ounces

2-inch piece of ginger root, peeled and grated

2 small red chilies, seeded and finely chopped

2 lemongrass sticks, finely chopped, with outer leaves removed

2 tablespoons vegetarian fish sauce

2 tablespoons light soy sauce

juice of 1 lime

1 teaspoon light brown sugar

2 tablespoons sesame seeds, toasted

6 ounces sugar-snap peas

1 red bell pepper, seeded and thinly sliced

1 carrot, cut into thin ribbons

8 kaffir lime leaves

4 scallions, sliced

¼ cup chopped cilantro leaves, plus extra to serve

1 Soak the banana leaves for a few minutes in warm water until pliable. Slice each tofu block into 4 pieces.

2 Mix together the ginger, chilies, lemongrass, fish sauce, soy sauce, lime juice, brown sugar, and sesame seeds in a bowl.

3 Spread the banana leaves out on a work surface and divide the peas, red pepper, and carrot in the middle of the leaves. Top each portion with 2 slices of the tofu. Spoon the ginger mixture over the top and top each portion with 2 kaffir lime leaves. Sprinkle with the scallions and cilantro.

4 Fold in the sides of each banana leaf and roll up to make a package. Secure each package with a piece of string, then steam in a two-tier bamboo steamer, or in batches in a regular steamer, 8 minutes.

5 Put each package on a serving plate and open carefully. Sprinkle with extra cilantro leaves and serve.

# ORANGE AND SQUASH TABBOULEH WITH HERBED FETA

**SERVES 4**

½ cup raisins

½ cup orange juice

1¼ cups bulgur wheat

1 teaspoon vegetable bouillon
   powder

2 tablespoons olive oil

1lb 10oz butternut squash, peeled,
   seeded and cut into bite-sized
   pieces

1 large onion, chopped

2 large garlic cloves, chopped

zest of 1 large orange

1 tablespoon ground sumac

1 large handful of cilantro leaves,
   chopped, plus extra to serve

salt and freshly ground black pepper

**BAKED FETA**

2 blocks of feta cheese, each about
   7 ounces, drained

2 tablespoons olive oil

2 tablespoons lemon thyme leaves

1 Soak the raisins in the orange juice about 30 minutes until soft. Meanwhile, make the baked feta. Preheat the oven to 350°F, then put each block of feta on a large piece of foil and sprinkle each one with half of the olive oil and half of the thyme. Season with pepper, then fold the foil over and seal to make two packages. Bake on a baking sheet 15 minutes, or until soft.

2 While the feta is baking, put the bulgur wheat in a heatproof bowl and cover with boiled water. Stir in the bouillon powder and set aside 5 minutes, then drain and transfer to a steamer basket lined with cheesecloth. Steam 10 minutes, or until tender, then set aside.

3 Heat the olive oil in a large skillet over medium-low heat and fry the squash 10 to 15 minutes, stirring occasionally, until tender and golden. Remove the squash from the pan, using a slotted spoon. Add the onion and fry 5 minutes, then stir in the garlic, orange zest, and sumac. Mix in the bulgur, squash, and orange juice and raisins and warm through. Season with salt and pepper and stir in the cilantro.

4 Divide the tabbouleh onto four plates. Open the feta parcels and cut each block of feta in half. Top each portion of tabbouleh with a piece of feta, sprinkle with extra cilantro, and serve.

# SOY-STEAMED TOFU WITH THAI BASIL

**SERVES 4**

2 tablespoons tamari soy sauce

6 tablespoons kecap manis

2 tablespoons sesame oil

1 pound 2 ounces firm tofu, patted
   dry and cut into wedges

¼ cup olive oil

1 long red chili, seeded and thinly
   sliced lengthwise

1½-inch piece of ginger root, peeled
   and sliced into thin strips

3 scallions, shredded

a few Thai basil leaves

1 In a shallow dish, mix together the tamari, kecap manis, and sesame oil. Add the tofu and spoon the marinade over it until coated. Let marinate at least 30 minutes.

2 Meanwhile, heat the olive oil in a small skillet over medium heat and fry the chili and ginger, stirring occasionally, until crisp. Drain on paper towels and set aside.

3 Remove the tofu from the marinade, using a spatula, and reserve the marinade. Put the tofu in a large steamer lined with baking parchment paper, cover, and steam 5 minutes.

4 Heat the reserved marinade in a small saucepan until warm. Carefully remove the tofu from the steamer and transfer to four plates. Spoon the marinade over the tofu, top with the scallions, basil, and crisp chili and ginger, and serve.

# MUSHROOM, CHESTNUT, AND PRUNE PUDDINGS

Traditionally British, suet pastry is the ultimate comfort food and is at its best when freshly cooked (by steaming or boiling). Prior to cooking the puddings, cover them with baking parchment paper and foil with a pleat down the middle to allow room for expansion.

**SERVES 4**

2 tablespoons olive oil, plus extra for greasing
1 large onion, chopped
1 large garlic clove, crushed
3 1/2 cups coarsely chopped Portobello mushrooms
2/3 cup chopped cooked chestnuts
1 teaspoon dried thyme
1/3 cup chopped prunes
1 1/4 cups dry red wine
1 tablespoon soy sauce
a few drops of hot-pepper sauce
salt and freshly ground black pepper

**VEGETABLE SUET PASTRY**

scant 1 1/2 cups self-rising flour, plus extra for kneading
a pinch of salt
3 1/2 ounces shredded vegetable suet

**RED WINE JUS**

1 cup dry red wine
1 cup vegetable stock
1 tablespoon balsamic vinegar
1 teaspoon granulated sugar
2 tablespoons butter

1 Lightly grease four 9-ounce pudding bowls with a little olive oil. Heat the oil in a large skillet over medium-low heat and cook the onion 8 minutes, or until soft. Add the garlic and mushrooms and cook 4 minutes, stirring often. Add the chestnuts, thyme, prunes, and wine and bring to a boil, then reduce the heat to low and simmer 5 to 8 minutes until the wine reduces and there is not any aroma of alcohol. Stir in the soy sauce and hot-pepper sauce, heat through, and season with salt and pepper, then let cool.

2 To make the pastry dough, sift the flour and salt into a mixing bowl. Stir in the suet, add 1/2 cup water, and mix to form a smooth, soft dough. Reserve one-quarter of the dough and roll out the remainder on a lightly floured surface to about 1/8 inch thick. Cut out 4 circles large enough to line each pudding bowl and leave a little overhang. Spoon the cooled mushroom mixture into the dough-lined bowls.

3 Roll out the remaining dough and cut out 4 circles to cover the tops of the puddings. Dampen the edges of the dough with water and lay the circles over the puddings. Press to seal, then trim any excess.

4 Cover each pudding with a piece of baking parchment paper, then a circle of foil (both with a pleat down the middle) and secure with string. Put the puddings in a large tiered steamer, cover, and steam 45 minutes, then carefully remove the puddings from the pan. (Check the water in the pan occasionally to make sure it is not running dry.) Run a knife around the edge of the puddings before turning them out.

5 While the puddings are cooking, make the red wine jus. Heat the red wine in a frying pan until boiling, then reduce the heat to medium-low and cook 10 minutes until it reduces by half. Add the stock, vinegar, and sugar and cook 5 minutes longer until thickened slightly. Remove the pan from the heat, stir in the butter to make a glossy sauce, and season with salt and pepper. Serve with the puddings.

# STUFFED SAVOY CABBAGE WITH CAULIFLOWER CREAM

Blanching the cabbage leaves first makes them flexible and easier to fold after filling them with the spicy potato and chickpea mixture.

**SERVES 4**

8 ounces potatoes, peeled and quartered, if large
8 large savoy cabbage leaves
2 tablespoons olive oil
1 large onion, finely chopped
1 large garlic clove, chopped
heaped 1 tablespoon peeled and chopped ginger root
1 teaspoon fenugreek seeds
2 teaspoons ground cumin
1 teaspoon ground coriander
½ teaspoon cayenne powder
1 tablespoon tamarind paste
1 cup cooked chickpeas, roughly mashed
1 carrot, grated
salt and freshly ground black pepper

**CAULIFLOWER CREAM**

3½ cups cauliflower florets
2 tablespoons olive oil
2 shallots, finely chopped
2 garlic cloves, chopped
1 cup plus 2 tablespoons vegetable stock
3 tablespoons crème fraîche or sour cream

1 Cook the potatoes in boiling salted water 10 to 12 minutes until tender. Drain them well, then cut them into small dice and transfer to a large bowl.

2 Meanwhile, steam the cauliflower 4 minutes, or until tender, then set aside. Bring a large saucepan of water to a boil. Cut a small v-shaped piece from the base of the stem of each cabbage leaf to make them easier to fold. Blanch the leaves 1 minute, or until flexible enough to fold without breaking. Drain and refresh under cold running water.

3 Heat the olive oil in a skillet over medium-low heat and fry the onion 8 minutes, or until soft. Add the garlic, ginger, fenugreek, cumin, coriander, and cayenne and cook 1 minute. Stir in the tamarind paste and 2 tablespoons water and heat through, then add the mixture to the potato. Add the chickpeas and carrot, mix well, and season well with salt and pepper.

4 Put 2 tablespoons of the potato mixture in the middle of each cabbage leaf. Fold the sides of each leaf over the filling, then roll up from the bottom to make 8 bundles.

5 Put the bundles, seam-side down, in a two-tiered steamer, cover, and steam 6 minutes until heated through. Or line a large steamer with baking parchment paper, cover, and steam the bundles in two batches; cover and keep warm while you cook the second batch.

6 To finish the cauliflower cream, heat the olive oil in a large sauté pan and sauté the shallots 5 minutes, or until soft. Add the garlic and cook 1 minute, then transfer to a blender. Add the cauliflower, stock, and crème fraîche and blend until smooth. Reheat slowly in the pan and season with salt and pepper.

7 To serve, divide the cauliflower cream onto four plates. Top each portion with 2 savoy cabbage bundles and season with black pepper.

# CREAMY PEA PUREE

**SERVES 4**
2 cups fresh or frozen petit pois
2 tablespoons crème fraîche or sour
cream
1 tablespoon olive oil
2 tablespoons chopped mint leaves,
plus extra to serve
1 teaspoon lemon juice
salt and freshly ground black pepper

1 Steam the peas 3 minutes, or until tender, then transfer them
to a blender.
2 Add the crème fraîche, olive oil, mint, lemon juice, and
2 tablespoons hot water and blend until pureed. Season with
salt and pepper, sprinkle with extra mint leaves, and serve warm.

# ARTICHOKES WITH LEMON AND GARLIC MAYO

When in season, artichokes are best eaten simply steamed with butter or
mayonnaise. Always use a stainless-steel knife and pan when preparing and
cooking artichokes, because iron and aluminum, including foil, will discolor them.
The mayonnaise in this recipe is made by hand but can also be prepared in a food
processor; it will keep up to five days in the refrigerator

**SERVES 4**
juice of ½ lemon
4 globe artichokes, rinsed

**LEMON AND GARLIC MAYO**
1 egg yolk, at room temperature
½ teaspoon English mustard
powder
7 tablespoons sunflower oil
1 teaspoon white wine vinegar
1 garlic clove, crushed
finely grated zest of ½ lemon
salt and freshly ground black pepper

1 First make the mayonnaise. In a mixing bowl, whisk together the
egg yolk and mustard powder. Season with salt and pepper, then
gradually whisk in the sunflower oil, adding just a few drops at
first and whisking until thoroughly incorporated. After a while,
you can add a greater quantity at a time, but make sure it's well
incorporated before adding more. Once all the oil is mixed in and the
mixture emulsifies and becomes thick, stir in the vinegar, garlic,
and lemon zest. Cover and chill the mayonnaise in the refrigerator
until ready to use.
2 To prepare the artichokes, fill a bowl with water and mix in the
lemon juice. Remove the tough outer leaves and cut off the stem
from each artichoke, taking care not to cut into the bottom. Cut off
the top ½ inch and then, using a pair of scissors, trim the outer
leaves. Dip the artichoke in the acidulated water to stop them from
discoloring. Repeat with the rest of the artichokes.
3 Fill the steamer pan with about 2 inches water and bring to a boil.
Put the artichokes in a single layer, stem-side down, in the steamer
basket, cover, and steam 20 to 35 minutes, depending on their size,
until tender and the leaves pull away easily. Remove the artichokes
with tongs and drain upside down in a colander. Serve warm or at
room temperature with the mayonnaise.

# CUMIN-SPIKED EGGPLANT

Eggplants are renowned for soaking up large quantities of oil during cooking, but steaming them helps to prevent this. And, surprisingly, they become meltingly tender when cooked this way.

**SERVES 4**

3 tablespoons olive oil
2 teaspoons cumin seeds
½ teaspoon dried chili flakes
4 tomatoes, seeded and diced
1 ¾ cups canned crushed tomatoes
juice of ½ lemon
2 tablespoons capers, drained and rinsed
1 handful of cilantro leaves, chopped
1 eggplant, peeled and cut into large chunks
2 large garlic cloves, peeled
salt and freshly ground black pepper

1 Toast the cumin seeds in a dry frying pan over medium heat 2 to 3 minutes, stirring occasionally, until lightly browned. Then remove from the heat and set aside.

2 Heat the olive oil in a sauté pan, add the cumin seeds and toast, stirring occasionally, 1 to 2 minutes or until they smell aromatic. Watch carefully so they do not burn. Add the chili flakes and the fresh and canned tomatoes and simmer, stirring occasionally, 10 minutes until reduced and thick. Stir in the lemon juice and capers, season with salt and pepper, and stir in the cilantro.

3 Meanwhile, put the eggplant and garlic in a steamer basket, cover, and steam 5 to 7 minutes until very tender, then lightly mash with a fork—the mixture should still be very chunky. Stir the eggplant and garlic into the tomato sauce and serve.

# GINGER AND MANGO COUSCOUS

**SERVES 4**

1 cup wholewheat couscous
3 tablespoons olive oil
juice of 1 lemon
1 garlic clove, crushed
1 tablespoon peeled and finely grated ginger root
1 long red chili, seeded and finely chopped
1 handful of cilantro leaves, chopped
1 handful of mint leaves, chopped
1 handful of fresh flat-leaf parsley leaves, chopped
1 mango, peeled, seeded, and diced
salt and freshly ground black pepper

1 Put the couscous in a heatproof bowl, cover with boiling water, and let soak 3 minutes, then drain. Transfer to a steamer lined with cheesecloth, cover, and steam 3 minutes, or until the grains are tender and fluffy. Transfer the couscous to a serving bowl.

2 Drizzle the olive oil and lemon juice over the couscous, then add the garlic, ginger, chili, cilantro, mint, and parsley. Stir until combined, then season with salt and pepper.

3 Stir the mango into the couscous and set aside to cool. Serve at room temperature.

# WARM GREEN BEAN SALAD

Dress the green beans while they're still warm and they will absorb the flavor of the oriental dressing more readily.

**SERVES 4**

9 ounces thin green beans, topped and tailed
¼ cup sunflower oil
2 large garlic cloves, thinly sliced
2-inch piece of ginger root, peeled and grated
1 tablespoon sesame oil
salt and freshly ground black pepper

1 Steam the green beans 5 minutes, or until tender, then arrange on a serving plate.
2 Meanwhile, heat the sunflower oil in a wok over medium-low heat. Add the garlic and stir-fry 2 minutes, or until light golden and starting to crisp. Remove from the wok with a slotted spoon and drain on paper towels.
3 Put the ginger in the middle of a piece of paper towel. Twist it into a bundle and squeeze to release the juices into a bowl. Add the sesame oil, season with salt and pepper, and pour the dressing over the green beans. Sprinkle with the garlic, then serve warm or at room temperature.

# LEMONGRASS AND GINGER RICE

This fragrant rice dish cooks for a short time in water and is then finished by the steam trapped inside the pan. Make sure the lid on the pan fits snuggly, or wrap the lid in a clean, dry dish towel to help trap the steam in the pan.

**SERVES 4**

1½ cups basmati rice
2 lemongrass sticks, crushed, with outer leaves removed
3 kaffir lime leaves
2 tablespoons sesame seeds
1 tablespoon sunflower oil
2 large garlic cloves, sliced
2¾-inch piece of ginger root, peeled and cut into matchsticks
2 tablespoons light soy sauce
2 teaspoons sesame oil

1 Put the rice and 3 cups water in a saucepan. Stir in the lemongrass and kaffir lime leaves and bring to a boil. Reduce the heat to low, cover with a tight-fitting lid, and simmer 10 to 12 minutes until the water is absorbed and the rice is tender. Do not remove the lid during the cooking or the steam will escape. Remove the pan from the heat and let stand 5 to 10 minutes.
2 Meanwhile, toast the sesame seeds in a dry skillet over medium heat 3 to 4 minutes, stirring occasionally, until lightly browned. Then remove from the heat and set aside.
3 Fluff up the rice with a fork. Heat the sunflower oil in a pan over medium-low heat and fry the garlic and ginger 1 minute. Add the soy sauce and sesame oil, then stir the mixture into the rice. Sprinkle the sesame seeds over the rice and serve.

# MANGO SUSHI

Fresh mango steeped in a ginger sugar syrup provides a sweet contrast to the sticky coconut rice. A wet knife makes the rice easier to cut and gives this dish a neater, more stylized presentation.

**MAKES 16 PIECES**

½ cup sushi rice, rinsed
⅔ cup canned coconut milk
½ teaspoon freshly grated nutmeg
6 tablespoons granulated sugar
1 mango
1 ½-inch piece of ginger root, peeled and thinly sliced

1 Put the rice in a saucepan and add enough water to just cover it. Bring to a boil and cook 3 minutes, or until beginning to soften, then drain well. Put the rice in a steamer lined with cheesecloth, cover, and steam 12 to 15 minutes until tender.

2 Carefully lift out the cheesecloth and transfer the rice to a heavy-bottomed saucepan. Add the coconut milk, nutmeg, and 2 tablespoons of the sugar and stir until combined. Bring to a boil, then reduce the heat to low and simmer 6 minutes, or until thick and creamy, stirring regularly to prevent the rice from sticking.

3 Line a small baking dish, about 10 x 7 inches, with plastic wrap, leaving enough overhanging the sides to cover the top when folded over. Spread the rice out to about ¾ inch thick and smooth the top with a wet metal spatula. Fold the overhanging plastic wrap over the top to cover and then let cool.

4 Peel the mango and slice thinly, discarding the seed. Cut the slices into 16 pieces, each 1 ½ x ¾ inch. Put the remaining sugar and ½ cup water in a small saucepan and stir over low heat until the sugar dissolves. Turn the heat up to medium and boil 2 minutes, or until reduced and syrupy. Remove the pan from the heat, add the ginger and mango slices, and let the syrup cool.

5 Lift the rice out of the baking dish and remove the plastic wrap. Using a wet knife, cut the rice into 16 pieces, each 1 ½ x ¾ inch. Arrange 1 piece of the mango on top of each rectangle of rice and arrange on a plate. Drizzle with the ginger syrup and serve.

# VANILLA–CINNAMON CUSTARD POTS WITH RHUBARB

**SERVES 6**

1¼ cups light cream

1 cup less 2 tablespoons milk

1 cinnamon stick

3 pieces star anise

1 teaspoon vanilla extract

3 eggs

5 tablespoons granulated sugar

dark brown sugar, to decorate

**GINGER RHUBARB**

14 ounces rhubarb, cut into bite-size
  pieces

6 tablespoons granulated sugar,
  or to taste

1 to 2 teaspoons ground ginger,
  to taste

1 Put the cream, milk, cinnamon stick, and star anise in a saucepan and heat until almost boiling. Reduce the heat to low and simmer 3 minutes, then turn off the heat, stir in the vanilla extract and let infuse at least 30 minutes. Meanwhile, make the ginger rhubarb. Put the rhubarb, sugar, ginger, and 3 tablespoons water in a nonreactive saucepan. Bring to a boil, then reduce the heat to low and simmer 7 minutes, or until soft.

2 Using an electric mixer, beat together the eggs and sugar until pale and creamy, then strain it into the cream mixture. Beat again, then equally divide among six ¾ -cup pots or ramekins.

3 Put the custards in a large steamer, cover, and steam 6 to 8 minutes until just set. Carefully remove the pots from the steamer.

4 If serving warm, sprinkle the custard pots with brown sugar and serve with the rhubarb. Or, let the custard pots cool, then chill 2 hours. Just before serving, sprinkle with brown sugar and serve with the rhubarb.

# CHOCOLATE PUDDINGS WITH MOCHA CREAM

**SERVES 4**

3 ounces dark chocolate, about
  70% cocoa solids, grated, plus
  extra to decorate

²/₃ cup milk

¼ cup less 1 teaspoon butter, plus
  extra for greasing

¼ cup granulated sugar

3 large eggs, separated

heaped 2 cups fresh white bread
  crumbs

1 teaspoon baking powder

**MOCHA CREAM**

2 tablespoons milk

1 tablespoon granulated sugar

1 tablespoon instant coffee granules

²/₃ cup heavy cream

1 Lightly grease four 9-ounce pudding bowls. Put the chocolate and milk in a heavy-bottomed saucepan and warm over low heat, stirring, until the chocolate melts.

2 Using an electric mixer, beat the butter and sugar 5 minutes, or until pale and fluffy. Beat in the egg yolks, then the chocolate mixture, bread crumbs, and baking powder. In a clean bowl, beat the egg whites until they form stiff peaks, then fold them into the chocolate mixture. Equally divide the mixture into the pudding bowls. Cover each with a circle of baking parchment paper, then with a circle of foil (both with a pleat down the middle). Secure with string and steam the puddings in a tiered steamer, or put them on an upturned plate in a large saucepan, adding enough water to come halfway up the sides of the bowls. Cover and steam 30 minutes, then set aside 5 minutes to firm up before turning out.

3 Meanwhile, make the mocha cream. Warm the milk and sugar in a small saucepan over medium-low heat, stirring, until the sugar dissolves. Dissolve the coffee in 1 tablespoon boiling water and add it to the pan. Transfer to a mixing bowl and let cool. In a separate bowl, beat the cream until soft peaks form, then stir it into the cooled coffee mixture. Serve the puddings with the mocha cream and a little extra chocolate grated over the tops.

# SWEET HAZELNUT AND CHOCOLATE BUNS

These light, fluffy, Chinese-style buns can be made the day before and reheated in a steamer when ready to eat. They can also be frozen and then defrosted before steaming.

**MAKES 16**

1½ teaspoons active dry yeast

2 tablespoons granulated sugar

2⅔ cups all-purpose flour, plus extra for kneading

1 teaspoon salt

1 tablespoon sunflower oil, plus extra for greasing

1½ teaspoons baking powder

**CHOCOLATE AND NUT FILLING**

heaped ¾ cup chocolate-hazelnut spread

3 tablespoons milk

¼ cup chopped toasted almonds

1 To make the dough, stir together the yeast, sugar, and 1 cup plus 2 tablespoons warm water in a small bowl until the sugar dissolves. Cover and let stand 10 minutes, or until frothy.

2 Sift the flour and salt into a mixing bowl and make a well in the middle. Pour the yeast mixture and sunflower oil into the well and gradually mix in the flour to form a soft ball of dough—it should be very sticky. Knead on a lightly floured surface 10 minutes, adding a little more flour if necessary, until smooth and elastic.

3 Grease a clean mixing bowl with oil, add the dough, and turn until coated. Cover with a clean, damp dish towel and let the dough rise in a warm place 2½ hours, or until double in size.

4 Turn the dough out onto a lightly floured surface, shape into ball, and sprinkle with the baking powder. Knead 5 minutes, then divide into 16 equal balls and cover with the damp dish towel.

5 Mix together the chocolate spread, milk, and almonds for the filling. Press a ball of dough into a circle about ¼ inch thick and put 1 heaped tablespoon of the chocolate mixture in the middle. Pull the edges up over the filling, press together to seal, and set aside on a lightly floured surface. Repeat to make 16 buns.

6 Put 4 or 5 buns in a large bamboo steamer lined with baking parchment paper, spacing them slightly apart (or use a two-tiered steamer, if you have one). Cover and steam over a wok of simmering water 15 minutes, or until risen and fluffy. If steaming in batches, cover the finished buns to keep warm while you cook the remaining ones. Replenish the steamer water as necessary to prevent it from boiling dry. Serve warm.

# DATE AND ORANGE PUDDING WITH MARMALADE SAUCE

There is nothing quite like an old fashioned British steamed pudding—a perfect dessert for a cold winter's day. Toward the end of the cooking time, check the water levels in the pan to make sure it is not boiling dry.

**SERVES 4**

6 tablespoons unsalted butter, plus extra for greasing

3 tablespoons golden syrup or maple syrup

2 tablespoons orange marmalade

juice of 2 oranges and finely grated zest of 1 orange

$^2/_3$ cup ready-to eat dried dates, coarsely chopped

$^2/_3$ cup self-rising flour

1 teaspoon baking soda

a pinch of salt

scant $^1/_2$ cup light brown sugar

3 large eggs

1 Lightly grease a 10-ounce pudding bowl with butter. In a small bowl, mix together the golden syrup and marmalade and spoon it into the bottom of the pudding bowl.

2 Put the orange juice, zest, and dates in a saucepan and bring to a boil, then reduce the heat to low and simmer 10 minutes, or until the dates are very soft. Mash them with a fork, then set aside to cool.

3 Sift together the flour, baking soda, and salt into a bowl. In another bowl, beat the butter and brown sugar with an electric mixer 2 minutes, or until light and fluffy. Beat in the eggs, one at a time, mixing well after each addition. Fold in the flour mixture, alternating with the mashed dates until well combined.

4 Pour the batter into the bowl and smooth the top. Cover with a circle of baking parchment paper, then with a circle of foil (both with a pleat down the middle) and secure with string. Put the bowl on a trivet or upturned saucer in a large saucepan. Add enough water to come halfway up the side of the bowl, cover with a tight-fitting lid, and bring to a boil. Reduce the heat to medium-low, cover, and steam 1 hour 15 minutes or until risen. A skewer inserted in the middle of the pudding should come out clean.

5 Carefully remove the bowl from the pan and let cool for a few minutes, then loosen with a knife, turn the pudding out onto a plate and serve.

Nurturing and nourishing, slow-simmered soups, stews, and curries are as good for the soul as they are for the body. Gentle simmering techniques allow the flavors of individual ingredients to mingle, while more vigorous boiling transforms foods such as pasta, noodles, and potatoes into the deliciously satisfying bases of many dishes.

# SIMMER

Watermelon Curry on Black Lentil Cakes, page 171

# SLOW-COOKED ONION AND CIDER SOUP WITH FONTINA CROUTES

Slow cooking tempers the pungency of the onions, making them sweet and meltingly tender.

**SERVES 4**

¼ cup olive oil

2 pounds 4 ounces onions, thinly sliced

leaves from 10 thyme sprigs, plus extra to serve

2 bay leaves

3 large garlic cloves, chopped

¾ cup hard cider or dry white wine

4 cups vegetable stock

1 tablespoon light soy sauce

salt and freshly ground black pepper

**FONTINA CROUTES**

4 thick slices of ciabatta bread, sliced diagonally

5 ounces Fontina cheese, rind removed and sliced

1 Heat the oil in a large saucepan over medium-low to low heat and cook the onions, partially covered, 35 minutes, stirring occasionally. Turning the heat to low if they start to brown too quickly. Remove the lid, then turn up the heat to medium and cook, stirring occasionally, 5 minutes longer, or until the onions start to color.

2 Add the thyme, bay leaves, garlic, and cider and bring to a boil. Boil 5 minutes or until the cider reduces by half. Add the stock and return to a boil, then stir, reduce the heat to low, and simmer, partially covered, 30 minutes.

3 Add the soy sauce and season with salt and pepper. If preferred, the soup can be partially pureed: pour half of the soup into a blender and blend, then return to the pan and reheat, if necessary.

4 To make the Fontina croutes, heat the broiler to medium-high. Lightly toast one side of each slice of bread under the broiler, then turn the slices over, top with the cheese, and broil until the cheese melts and is bubbling.

5 Ladle the soup into bowls and top with the croutes. Sprinkle with a little extra thyme and serve immediately.

# VEGETABLE, NORI, AND NOODLE RAMEN

**SERVES 4**

2 large eggs, at room temperature
6 ounces ramen noodles
1 tablespoon sunflower oil
2 leeks, thinly sliced
2 zucchini, thinly sliced diagonally
2 cups sliced button mushrooms
3 handfuls of spinach leaves, shredded
2½ cups sliced Chinese cabbage leaves
6½ cups vegetable stock
3 tablespoons light soy sauce
2 tablespoons grated peeled ginger root
1 teaspoon sesame oil
2 scallions, finely chopped
¼ teaspoon dried chili flakes
4 toasted nori strips, crumbled

1 Put the eggs in a saucepan of boiling water. Return to a boil, then reduce the heat to low and simmer 6 minutes. Remove from the pan from the heat and rinse under cold running water 1 minute. Set aside until cool enough to handle, then peel and halve lengthwise.

2 Meanwhile, bring a large saucepan of water to a boil. Stir in the noodles to immerse them in the water and separate the strands. Return to a boil and cook over medium-high heat 4 minutes or until tender. Drain and divide the noodles into four bowls.

3 While the noodles are cooking, heat the sunflower oil in a large saucepan over medium-low heat and cook the leeks, zucchini, and mushrooms 2 minutes, then add the spinach and Chinese leaves and stir-fry 1 minute longer. Add the stock, soy sauce, and ginger and bring to a boil, then reduce the heat to low and stir in the sesame oil. Heat through until the noodles have finished cooking.

4 Scoop out the vegetables from the soup with a slotted spoon and add to the bowls of noodles. Pour enough stock into each bowl to fill, then sprinkle with scallions, chili flakes, and nori. Top each bowl with half a hard-boiled egg and serve immediately.

# COCONUT, LENTIL, AND CHILI SOUP

**SERVES 4**

2 tablespoons sunflower oil
2 onions, finely chopped
2 teaspoons coriander seeds, crushed
1 chili, split in half lengthwise
2 garlic cloves, chopped
1 tablespoon peeled and grated ginger root
1 lemongrass stick, finely chopped, with outer leaves removed
1 cup dried red lentils, rinsed
4 cups vegetable stock
1 tablespoon tomato paste
1¾ cups canned coconut milk
juice of 1 lime
¼ cup cilantro leaves, chopped
2 scallions, finely chopped
salt and freshly ground black pepper

1 Heat the oil in a large saucepan over medium-low heat and fry the onions 8 minutes or until soft. Add the coriander seeds, chili, garlic, ginger, and lemongrass and cook 1 minute longer.

2 Add the lentils and stir to coat them in the oil and spices, then add the stock and bring to a boil. Reduce the heat to low and simmer, partially covered, 20 minutes. Stir in the tomato paste and coconut milk and continue simmering 15 to 20 minutes until the lentils are soft and breaking down into the soup.

3 Add the lime juice and 3 tablespoons of the cilantro leaves and season to taste with salt and pepper. Ladle the soup into four bowls, sprinkle with the remaining cilantro leaves and scallions, then serve immediately.

# JERUSALEM ARTICHOKE SOUP

Quirky, oddly shaped Jerusalem artichokes make a remarkably good, thick soup, thanks to their mildly nutty flavor. The truffle oil is an optional decadence.

**SERVES 4**

2 tablespoons olive oil
1 large onion, chopped
1 celery stick, chopped
1 carrot, sliced
1 large garlic clove, chopped
1 pound 8 ounces Jerusalem
   artichokes, scrubbed or peeled,
   and chopped
5 cups vegetable stock
1 cup plus 2 tablespoons milk
4 thick slices of sourdough bread,
   crusts removed
truffle oil, for drizzling (optional)
½ cup grated Parmesan cheese
salt and freshly ground black pepper

1  Heat the oil in a large saucepan over medium-low heat and sauté the onion 6 minutes or until soft. Add the celery, carrot, garlic, and Jerusalem artichokes and sauté 5 minutes longer, stirring occasionally.

2  Add the stock and bring to a boil, then reduce the heat to low and simmer 25 minutes, stirring occasionally, or until the vegetables are tender. Using an immersion blender, puree the soup until smooth. Stir in the milk, season with salt and pepper, and warm through.

3  Meanwhile, toast the slices of bread, then cut them into cubes. Spoon the soup into four bowls, then top with the croutons and drizzle with a little truffle oil, if using. Sprinkle a heap of the Parmesan into the middle and serve.

# SPICED APPLE AND PARSNIP SOUP WITH PARSNIP CRISPS

**SERVES 4**

5 parsnips, peeled
6 tablespoons sunflower oil
1 large onion, chopped
1 celery stick, thinly sliced
1 bay leaf
1 teaspoon ground cumin
1 teaspoon ground coriander
½ teaspoon turmeric
½ to 1 teaspoon dried chili flakes
4 cups vegetable stock
2 slightly sharp apples, peeled,
   cored and diced
2 teaspoons lemon juice
salt and freshly ground black pepper

1  Slice 4 of the parsnips and use a vegetable peeler, to cut the remaining parsnip lengthwise into thin ribbons.

2  Heat 1 tablespoon of the sunflower oil in a large saucepan and cook the onion, partially covered, 6 minutes, stirring occasionally, until soft. Add the celery, sliced parsnips, bay leaf, cumin, coriander, turmeric, and chili flakes and cook 2 minutes, stirring regularly. Add the stock and bring to a boil, then reduce the heat to medium-low. Cook, partially covered, 10 minutes, stirring occasionally.

3  Add the apples and cook 6 to 8 minutes longer until soft, then stir in the lemon juice. Using an immersion blender, puree the soup until smooth. Taste and add more chili, if desired, then season with salt and pepper.

4  Heat the remaining oil in a skillet and fry the parsnip ribbons 2 to minutes or until crisp and golden. Drain on paper towels.

5  Reheat the soup and ladle it into four bowls. Top with the crisp parsnip ribbons and serve.

# WAKAME, RADISH, AND NOODLE SALAD

**SERVES 4**

¾ ounce dried wakame, cut into
    small pieces or strips
2 tablespoons pumpkin seeds,
    toasted
3 ounces vermicelli rice noodles
1¾ cups thinly sliced radishes
1 small cucumber, seeded and cut
    into thin ribbons
¾ cup peeled daikon cut into
    matchsticks
2 tablespoons pink pickled ginger
2 tablespoons shiso sprouts or
    radish sprouts

**SESAME–MIRIN DRESSING**

2 tablespoons sunflower or canola
    oil
1 tablespoon sesame oil
2 tablespoons light soy sauce
3 tablespoons rice wine vinegar
2 tablespoons mirin
1 tablespoon finely grated peeled
    ginger root
salt and freshly ground black pepper

1 Soak the wakame in a bowl of warm water 10 to 15 minutes until rehydrated. Drain, rinse under cold running water, and drain again.
2 Meanwhile, toast the pumpkin seeds in a dry skillet over medium-low heat 3 to 4 minutes, stirring frequently. Watch carefully as they easily burn.
3 Put the noodles in a heatproof bowl and soak in boiled water 3 to 5 minutes until soft. Rinse them, then refresh them under cold running water. Put the noodles, wakame, radishes, cucumber, and daikon in a bowl.
4 Mix together all of the ingredients for the dressing, pour it over the salad and toss lightly until combined.
5 Divide the salad into four bowls and sprinkle with the pumpkin seeds. Arrange the pickled ginger and shiso sprouts in a heap on top and serve.

# SHAOXING TOFU WITH STAR ANISE

**SERVES 4**

1 tablespoon sesame oil
1-inch piece of ginger root peeled
    and cut into matchsticks
½ cup Shaoxing wine
2 star anise
¼ cup hoisin sauce
2 tablespoons dark soy sauce
14 ounces firm tofu, patted dry and
    cut into ½-inch-thick slices
2 scallions, thinly sliced diagonally

1 Heat a large wok over medium-high heat. Add the sesame oil and the ginger and fry, stirring occasionally, 1 minute. Add the Shaoxing wine and cook 2 to 3 minutes until it reduces by half, then stir in the star anise, hoisin sauce, soy sauce, and tofu.
2 Reduce the heat to low and simmer 5 minutes, occasionally spooning the sauce over the tofu. Using a spatula, remove the tofu from the wok and set aside. Increase the heat to medium-low and cook the sauce 2 to 3 minutes until it reduces and is thick.
3 Divide the tofu between four shallow bowls and spoon the sauce over it. Sprinkle with the scallions and serve.

# MUSTARD AND LEMON PUY LENTILS WITH ZA'ATAR EGGS

Za'atar is a Middle Eastern condiment made from herbs, sesame seeds, salt and sometimes other spices. It is often mixed with olive oil and used as a spread on bread, a seasoning, or, as here, a coating.

**SERVES 4**

1¼ cups Puy lentils
2 bay leaves
4 eggs, at room temperature
2 tablespoons olive oil
1 large onion, chopped
1 celery stick, finely sliced
1 large red bell pepper, seeded and diced
3 large garlic cloves, chopped
6 plum tomatoes, seeded and diced
7 tablespoons vegetable stock, hot
juice of 1 lemon
finely grated zest of ½ lemon
1 tablespoon Dijon mustard
heaped ¼ cup crème fraîche or sour cream
¼ cup chopped flat-leaf parsley leaves
freshly ground black pepper

**ZA'ATAR SPICE MIX**

1 tablespoon sesame seeds
1 tablespoon ground sumac
2 tablespoons thyme leaves
1 teaspoon salt, crushed, plus extra to taste

1 Put the lentils and bay leaves in a saucepan, cover with water, and bring to a boil. Reduce the heat to low and simmer, partially covered, 25 minutes or until the lentils are tender, then drain.

2 Meanwhile, put the eggs in a small saucepan of boiling water. Return the water to a boil, then reduce the heat to a simmer, and cook the eggs 6 minutes. Remove the eggs from the pan and rinse them under cold running water 1 minute to prevent them cooking farther, then set aside.

3 Heat the olive oil in a large skillet and fry the onion 10 minutes, stirring occasionally, until soft and golden. Add the celery and red pepper and fry 3 minutes, then add the garlic and cook 1 minute longer, stirring occasionally. Stir in the tomatoes, stock, lemon juice, lemon zest, mustard, crème fraîche, and lentils. Cook 2 to 3 minutes until warmed through and the tomatoes are starting to soften.

4 Meanwhile, to make the za'atar spice mix, toast the sesame seeds in a dry skillet over medium heat 2 to 3 minutes, stirring often, until lightly browned. Remove from the heat and mix with the remaining za'atar ingredients in a small bowl. Peel the eggs and roll them in the za'atar. (Store any leftover za'atar in an airtight jar up to three weeks.)

5 Season the lentils with salt and pepper and stir in the parsley, then divide them into four large, shallow bowls. Cut the eggs in half lengthwise, put 2 halves on top of each portion of lentils and serve.

# SPRING VEGETABLE AND LEMON TAGLIATELLE

**SERVES 4**

13 ounces dried egg tagliatelle

10 ounces asparagus tips

2 zucchini, sliced into long vertical strips, then halved lengthwise

4 scallions, sliced diagonally

juice of 1 small lemon

7 ounces rindless goat cheese, crumbled

salt and freshly ground black pepper

basil leaves, to serve

### GARLIC CRUMBS

5 tablespoons olive oil

2 cups fresh bread crumbs

2 large garlic cloves, finely chopped

finely grated zest of 1 small lemon

1 red chili, seeded and sliced

1 First make the garlic crumbs. Heat 2 tablespoons of the olive oil in a skillet over medium heat and fry the bread crumbs 2 minutes, stirring occasionally, until beginning to crisp. Add the garlic, lemon zest, and chili and cook 2 to 3 minutes longer until the crumbs are golden, then set aside.

2 Cook the tagliatelle according to the package directions until al dente, then drain, reserving ½ cup of the cooking water. Meanwhile, steam the asparagus and zucchini 3 to 5 minutes, or until just tender, then refresh under cold running water.

3 Heat the rest of the olive oil in a large skillet over medium-low heat and fry the scallions 1 minute, stirring occasionally. Add the cooked pasta and reserved cooking water and turn until coated. Add the zucchini, asparagus, lemon juice, and half of the garlic crumbs and warm through, tossing well. Season with salt and pepper.

4 Divide the tagliatelle onto four plates and top with the goat cheese and remaining garlic crumbs. Scatter with torn basil leaves over and serve.

# RED QUINOA AND SPINACH SALAD WITH PECANS AND HALLOUMI

**SERVES 4**

¾ cup red quinoa

9 ounces halloumi cheese, sliced

olive oil, for brushing

2 tablespoons ras-el-hanout

½ cup pecan halves

¼ cup pumpkin seeds

2 large handfuls of baby leaf spinach

6 unsulfured dried apricots, chopped

1 small red onion, thinly sliced

¼ cup chopped flat-leaf parsley leaves

### POMEGRANATE DRESSING

3 tablespoons pomegranate molasses

1 tablespoon lemon juice

3 tablespoons olive oil

1 garlic clove, crushed

½ teaspoon granulated sugar

a pinch of ground cumin

salt and freshly ground black pepper

1 Put the quinoa in a saucepan and cover with water. Bring to a boil, then reduce the heat to low and simmer, covered, 10 to 15 minutes until tender. Drain well and set aside to cool in a bowl.

2 Brush the halloumi with olive oil and dust it in the ras-el-hanout. Heat a griddle pan over high heat until it almost starts to smoke. Reduce the heat to medium and griddle the halloumi 3 to 4 minutes, turning once, until the griddle marks are visible but the cheese still remains a little soft.

3 Meanwhile, toast the pecans in a single layer in a dry skillet over medium-low heat 2 to 3 minutes, turning halfway through. Remove from the pan and repeat with the pumpkin seeds.

4 In a small bowl, mix together all of the ingredients for the dressing and add it to the quinoa. Add the spinach, apricots, red onion, and parsley and toss until coated. Divide onto four plates and top with the pecans, pumpkin seeds, and halloumi and serve.

# BHEL PURI ON POPPADOM CRISPS

This delicious Indian-inspired salad is a perfect example of how you can transform simple ingredients into something very special. Some brands of tamarind paste contain the seeds; if so, pick them out before use.

**SERVES 4**

1 pound new potatoes, halved
1½ cups cooked chickpeas
2 red chilies, seeded and chopped
1 small red onion, finely chopped
heaped ¼ cup chopped cilantro
   leaves
4 uncooked poppadoms
sunflower oil, for frying
4 tomatoes, seeded and diced
salt and freshly ground black pepper

**TAMARIND AND YOGURT DRESSING**

3 tablespoons tamarind paste
1-inch piece of ginger root, peeled
   and finely chopped
½ teaspoon ground cumin
1 tablespoon lemon juice
5 tablespoons plain yogurt

1  Cook the potatoes in boiling salted water 10 minutes or until tender. Drain and set aside until cool enough to handle, then peel off the skins. Dice the potatoes and transfer to a bowl. Add the chickpeas, chilies, red onion, and 3 tablespoons of the cilantro leaves. Season with salt and pepper.

2  Put all of the ingredients for the dressing and 1 tablespoon water in a food processor and process until almost smooth. Pour the dressing over the potato salad and mix gently until well combined. Set aside.

3  To cook the poppadoms, heat 2 inches of the oil in a wide saucepan over medium-high heat until it reaches 375°F, or until a cube of bread turns golden in 20 seconds when dropped in the oil. Cook the poppadoms, one at a time, holding them under the oil with a metal spatula 2 to 3 seconds, or until puffed and crisp. Drain well on paper towels.

4  To serve, put each poppadom on a plate and pile one-quarter of the potato salad on top of each one. Top with the tomatoes and remaining cilantro leaves and serve at room temperature.

# WINTER VEGETABLE AND COFFEE STEW WITH CHEESE DUMPLINGS

The intensity of the coffee in this recipe lends a depth and richness to the stock, without being overpowering in flavor.

**SERVES 4**

2 tablespoons olive oil

2 onions, chopped

1 celery stick, sliced

1 leek, sliced

2 turnips, peeled and cut into
bite-size pieces

2 parsnips, peeled and cut into
bite-size pieces

9 ounces baby carrots, trimmed

1 cup sliced shiitake mushrooms

1 tablespoon all-purpose flour

6 thyme sprigs

1 bay leaf

scant 1 cup strong brewed coffee

1 cup plus 2 tablespoons vegetable
stock

2 tablespoons dark soy sauce

1 ½ cups cooked borlotti beans

salt and freshly ground black pepper

CHEESE DUMPLINGS

heaped ½ cup self-rising flour

⅓ cup grated sharp cheddar cheese

2 tablespoons chopped parsley
leaves

3 tablespoons soft butter, cut into
small pieces

1 Heat the oil in a large flameproof casserole over medium-low heat and fry the onions 6 minutes, stirring occasionally, until soft. Add the celery and leek and sauté 2 minutes, then add the turnips, parsnips, carrots, and shiitake mushrooms. Stir in the flour and cook 1 minute, stirring, then add the thyme and bay leaf. Add the coffee, stock, soy sauce, and borlotti beans and bring to a boil, then reduce the heat to low and simmer 10 minutes, stirring occasionally. Season with salt and pepper.

2 Meanwhile, make the dumplings. Mix together the flour, cheddar, parsley, and butter in a bowl. Stir in 1 tablespoon water and bring the mixture together with your hands to make a firm ball of dough. Divide the dough into 8 equal pieces and shape them into balls.

3 Arrange the dumplings in the casserole so they are half submerged in the vegetable mixture. Cover the casserole with a lid and simmer over low heat 20 to 25 minutes until the dumplings rise and the vegetables are tender. Serve hot.

# MUSHROOM AND CHESTNUT RAGOUT WITH SWEET POTATO MASH

Simmered over low heat, the mushrooms really absorb the flavors of the sherry and soy to produce a dark, potent stew with a rich, earthy taste.

**SERVES 4**

1 1/2 ounces dried porcini
   mushrooms
3 tablespoons olive oil
3 tablespoons butter
12 ounces shallots, peeled and
   halved with the root ends intact,
   or quartered if large
7 cups thickly sliced portobello
   mushrooms
2 teaspoons dried thyme
1/2 cup dry sherry
heaped 2 cups thickly sliced cooked
   chestnuts
2 tablespoons light soy sauce
a few splashes of hot-pepper sauce
5 tablespoons heavy cream
a few sprigs parsley leaves, chopped
salt and freshly ground black pepper

**SWEET POTATO MASH**

2 pounds sweet potatoes, peeled
   and cut into chunks
2 large garlic cloves
2/3 cup milk
2 tablespoons butter

**1** Soak the porcini mushrooms in 2/3 cup boiled water 20 minutes, or until soft.

**2** Heat the olive oil and butter in a large, heavy-bottomed saucepan over medium-low heat and cook the shallots 12 minutes, stirring regularly, until soft and golden in places. Add the portobello mushrooms and cook 4 to 5 minutes until tender.

**3** Strain the porcini mushrooms, reserving the soaking liquid, and add them to the pan, along with the thyme and sherry. Bring to a boil, then reduce the heat to low and simmer until the liquid reduces by half and there is not any more aroma of alcohol.

**4** Add the porcini soaking liquid, chestnuts, soy sauce, and hot-pepper sauce and simmer 10 to 15 minutes or until the liquid reduces by half. Stir in the cream and heat through gently, then season with salt and pepper.

**5** Meanwhile, make the sweet potato mash. Cook the sweet potatoes and garlic in boiling salted water 10 minutes or until tender, then drain the potatoes and return them to the pan. Add the milk and butter, season well with salt and pepper, and warm through. Mash mash the potatoes until smooth, then cover with a lid to keep warm.

**6** Sprinkle the ragout with the parsley and serve with the sweet potato mash.

# SPLIT PEA AND PANEER CURRY

Split peas benefit from long, slow cooking to give them time to break down and thicken the sauce. This curry can be made up to three days in advance then reheated, which allows the flavors to meld and intensify.

**SERVES 4**

1 cup yellow split peas, rinsed
3 tablespoons sunflower oil
2 onions, finely chopped
3 garlic cloves, chopped
2-inch piece of ginger root, peeled and grated
2 teaspoons yellow mustard seeds
2 teaspoons cumin seeds
1 teaspoon fennel seeds
1 large red chili, seeded and chopped
1 teaspoon turmeric
1 teaspoon ground coriander
2 carrots, diced
3 curry leaf sprigs
scant 1 cup tomato puree
1¼ cups vegetable stock
1¼ cups canned coconut milk
8 ounces paneer cheese, cubed
salt and freshly ground black pepper
cilantro leaves, to serve

1 Put the yellow split peas in a large saucepan and cover with plenty of water. Bring to a boil, then reduce the heat to low and simmer, partially covered, 40 minutes or until tender. Occasionally skim off any foam that rises to the surface. Drain the split peas and return them to the pan.

2 Heat the sunflower oil in a large skillet over medium-low heat and fry the onions 10 minutes until soft and turning golden. Stir in the garlic, ginger, and mustard, cumin, and fennel seeds and cook 2 minutes, then stir in the chili, turmeric, and ground coriander. Add the mixture to the pan with the split peas.

3 Add the carrots, curry leaves, tomato puree, and stock. Bring to a boil, then reduce the heat to low and simmer, partially covered, 10 minutes. Stir in the coconut milk and paneer and simmer, stirring occasionally, 10 minutes longer, or until thick. Season with salt and pepper, then sprinkle with cilantro leaves and serve.

# GNOCCHI WITH SQUASH AND TOASTED WALNUTS IN SAGE BUTTER

There are many versions of gnocchi, depending on where you are in Italy. The ratio of potato to flour, as well as the inclusion of egg vary greatly as does the shape and size of these little pasta dumplings, literally translated as "little lumps."

**SERVES 4**

1 ¼ cups even-size Idaho potatoes, unpeeled

1 ½ cups Italian 00 flour or regular all-purpose flour, plus extra for rolling

1 large egg, lightly beaten

salt and freshly ground black pepper

freshly grated Parmesan or pecorino cheese, to serve

**SAUCE**

4 ¾ cups peeled and seeded butternut squash cut into bite-size chunks

6 tablespoons olive oil

1 ¼ cups walnut halves

5 tablespoons butter

1 small handful of sage leaves, coarsely chopped

1 Cook the potatoes in boiling water 20 minutes or until tender. Drain well and when they are cool enough to handle, peel off the skins. Sift the flour into a bowl, make a well in the middle, and add the egg. Grate the potatoes (or press them through a strainer or food mill) onto the flour and egg. Season with salt and mix thoroughly, kneading to make a soft dough—you might need to add a little extra flour.

2 With floured hands, roll the dough into a rope shape, about ⅝ inch in diameter and then cut into ¾-inch pieces. Press a finger into each piece to flatten slightly, then draw your finger toward you to curl the side. Chill the gnocchi until you are ready to cook.

3 Meanwhile, roast the squash for the sauce. Preheat the oven to 400°F and grease a baking tray with 1 tablespoon of the olive oil. Roast the squash 20 minutes or until tender, turning halfway. Put the walnuts on a clean baking sheet and bake 3 to 5 minutes until toasted. Let cool slightly, then chop coarsely.

4 Bring a large saucepan of salted water to a boil and cook the gnocchi, about 20 at a time, 2 to 3 minutes until they float to the top. Remove from the water using a slotted spoon and transfer to a plate. Cover to keep warm while you cook the remaining gnocchi.

5 Heat the remaining oil and butter in a large saucepan over medium-low heat. Fry the sage 1 minute, stirring, then add the squash and half of the walnuts. Stir in the cooked gnocchi and gently turn until coated, adding a splash of water if too dry. Sprinkle with the reserved walnuts and Parmesan and serve.

# EGGPLANT, APRICOT, AND ALMOND TAGINE

The word "tagine" refers both to the earthenware cooking pot with a shallow bottom and conical lid and the Moroccan stew that is cooked in it. There are numerous versions of a tagine, but the essence of the dish is that it is simmered slowly and gently to create an intensely flavored aromatic sauce. The addition of dried apricots here lends a rich sweetness to the stew, while the spice mix ras-el-hanout guarantees an authentic flavor. Serve with couscous.

**SERVES 4**

2 tablespoons olive oil
2 tablespoons butter
1 large onion, sliced
1 large eggplant, cut into 1-inch
  cubes
2 large garlic cloves, chopped
2 zucchini, thickly sliced
2 tablespoons ras-el-hanout
½ teaspoon dried chili flakes
1 ½ cups peeled sweet potatoes cut
  into 1-inch cubes
2 ½ cups tomato puree
1 tablespoon tomato paste
1 tablespoon honey
1 cup dried apricots
1 ½ cups cooked chickpeas
⅓ cup whole blanched almonds
salt and freshly ground black pepper
1 small handful of cilantro leaves,
  chopped, to serve

1 Heat the olive oil and butter in a tagine or large, wide saucepan over medium heat. Add the onion and sauté over medium-low heat 6 minutes, stirring regularly. Add the eggplant, garlic, and zucchini and cook 5 minutes longer, stirring occasionally, or until the vegetables are soft.

2 Add the ras-el-hanout and stir until the vegetables are coated in the spices. Add the dried chili flakes, sweet potatoes, tomato puree, tomato paste, honey, and ⅔ cup water and bring to a boil, then stir until combined and reduce the heat to low.

3 Simmer, covered, 15 minutes, stirring occasionally, until the sauce begins to thicken. Stir in the apricot and chickpeas, cover again, and cook 15 minutes longer, or until the vegetables are tender. Add a little water if the tagine is too dry. Season with salt and pepper

4 Meanwhile, preheat the oven to 350°F. Put the almonds on a baking sheet and bake 5 to 6 minutes until toasted. Remove from the oven and set aside to cool.

5 Sprinkle the tagine with the cilantro leaves and toasted almonds and serve.

# MINTED PEA AND LEEK RISOTTO WITH SOFT POACHED EGG

The secret to a good risotto is firstly the right rice: use arborio, carnaroli or vialone as they give a wonderful creamy, velvety texture when cooked, yet the grain retains a little bite in the middle. Equally important is adding the stock gradually and gently stirring until it is absorbed.

**SERVES 4**

2 tablespoons olive oil
2 leeks, finely chopped
1 ¾ cups arborio rice
⅔ cup dry white wine
2 cups frozen petit pois
1 handful of mint leaves, chopped
1 handful of basil leaves, plus extra
   to serve
6 ½ cups vegetable stock, hot
1 cup finely grated Parmesan
   cheese, plus extra to serve
4 large eggs
salt and freshly ground black pepper

1 Heat the olive oil in a large, heavy-bottomed saucepan over medium heat. Add the leeks, cover, and reduce the heat to medium-low. Cook 5 minutes, stirring occasionally, or until soft. Add the rice and stir 2 minutes to coat it in the oil. Add the wine and bring to a boil over medium-high heat, then reduce the heat to medium-low and cook until it is absorbed by the rice.

2 Meanwhile, steam the peas 3 minutes until tender, then transfer to a blender. Add the mint, basil, and scant ½ cup of the stock and blend until pureed, then set aside.

3 Add a ladleful of hot stock to the rice and cook, stirring continuously with a wooden spoon, until the rice absorbs the liquid. Continue to add the stock, a ladleful at a time, stirring to allow the rice to cook evenly and to prevent it from sticking to the pan, until all the stock is used and the rice is cooked and creamy, but still retains a slight bite. This will take about 25 minutes. Remove the pan from the heat and stir in the pea puree and Parmesan.

4 Bring a large sauté pan of water to a boil, then reduce the heat to low. Break 1 egg into a cup and then slip it out of the cup into the water. Repeat with the 3 remaining eggs and simmer 3 to 5 minutes, occasionally spooning the water over the top of each one, until the white is set but the yolk remains soft.

5 While the eggs are cooking, warm through the risotto, then season with salt and pepper. Divide the risotto into four shallow bowls and top with a poached egg. Sprinkle with extra Parmesan and basil leaves and serve immediately.

# WATERMELON CURRY ON BLACK LENTIL CAKES

Watermelon makes a wonderfully vibrant, fresh tasting curry. Toast the whole spices first in a dry skillet to enrich the flavor of the sauce.

**SERVES 4**

1 ½ -inch piece of ginger root, peeled
2 large garlic cloves, chopped
1 tablespoon sunflower oil
2 teaspoons cumin seeds
1 teaspoon fenugreek seeds
1 long red chili, seeded and finely chopped
5 pounds watermelon, peeled, seeded, and cut into bite-size chunks
2 teaspoons turmeric
2 teaspoons ground coriander
2 tablespoons lime juice
2 tablespoons shredded mint leaves
salt and freshly ground black pepper

**BLACK LENTIL CAKES**

1 ¼ cups whole black lentils
1 tablespoon sunflower oil, plus extra for frying
1 large onion, finely chopped
2 large garlic cloves, chopped
2 teaspoons cumin seeds
2 teaspoons garam masala
2 teaspoons ground coriander
1 teaspoon hot chili powder
1 egg, lightly beaten
3 tablespoons all-purpose flour, plus extra for coating

1  First make the black lentil cakes. Put the lentils in a saucepan, cover with water, and bring to a boil. Reduce the heat to low and simmer, partially covered, 40 minutes or until the lentils are very tender. Drain the lentils, then transfer them to a mixing bowl and roughly mash with a potato masher or the back of a fork. Set aside to cool.

2  Meanwhile, heat the sunflower oil for the lentil cakes in a skillet over medium-low heat and fry the onion 8 minutes, stirring occasionally, until soft. Add the garlic and cumin and cook 1 minute. Stir in the garam masala, coriander, and chili powder, then add the mixture to the bowl with the lentils. Stir in the egg and flour and season well with salt and pepper.

3  With floured hands, divide the lentil mixture into 4 equal portions and shape each one into a cake, then lightly coat each one in a little flour. The mixture is quite loose, so press the cake firmly until it holds its shape—the flour will help to achieve this. Put the cakes on a plate and chill until ready to cook.

4  To make the watermelon curry, puree the ginger and garlic in a food processor until they form a paste. Heat the sunflower oil in a skillet over medium heat and fry the paste 1 minute, stirring occasionally. Stir in the cumin and fenugreek seeds and cook 1 minute longer, then add the red chili.

5  Puree half of the watermelon in the food processor and add it to the skillet along with the turmeric and coriander. Bring to a boil, then reduce the heat to low and simmer 10 minutes, or until reduced by half and thick.

6  Meanwhile, cook the lentil cakes. Heat enough oil to generously coat a large, nonstick skillet over medium heat. Add the cakes, flattening slightly with a metal spatula, and fry 2 to 3 minutes on each side until crisp.

7  Add the lime juice and remaining watermelon to the curry and season with salt and pepper. Cook 5 to 8 minutes longer until soft.

8  Put 1 lentil cake on each of four plates and top with the watermelon curry. Sprinkle with the mint and serve.

# BLACK BEAN MOLE WITH CHICKPEA PANCAKES

There are numerous versions of the classic Mexican mole sauce, spiked with chili, spices, and a hint of dark chocolate. While the chipotle chili is not strictly authentic, it lends a delicious smokiness and hint of tobacco.

**SERVES 4**

3 ½ cups peeled and seeded acorn squash cut into bite-size chunks

3 tablespoons blanched almonds

2 tablespoons olive oil

1 large onion, chopped

3 garlic cloves, chopped

1 dried chipotle chili, finely chopped or 3 tablespoons chipotle paste

1 dried ancho chili, finely chopped

½ to 1 teaspoon dried chili flakes

2 teaspoons paprika

½ teaspoon cinnamon

1 teaspoon ground cumin

½ teaspoon ground allspice

2 ½ cupsw tomato puree

2 bay leaves

2 teaspoons dark brown sugar

1 ½ ounces dark chocolate, chopped

2 cups cooked black beans

finely grated zest of ½ lime, plus extra to serve

6 tablespoons crème fraîche or sour cream

salt and freshly ground black pepper

1 avocado, to serve

**CHICKPEA PANCAKES**

2 ½ cups chickpea flour

1 teaspoon baking soda

1 teaspoon salt

sunflower oil, for frying

1 To make the chickpea pancakes, sift the chickpea flour, baking soda, and salt into a large mixing bowl. Make a well in the middle and pour in 1 ¾ cups water. Gradually whisk the flour into the water to make a smooth batter. Let stand 20 minutes or until ready to cook.

2 Steam the squash 6 minutes or until tender, then set aside. Meanwhile, toast the almonds in a dry skillet over medium-low heat 3 to 4 minutes, then set aside to cool.

3 Heat the olive oil in a large pan over medium-low heat and fry the onion 8 minutes or until soft. Add the garlic, chipotle, ancho, chili flakes, paprika, cinnamon, cumin, and allspice and cook 2 minutes, stirring. Add the tomato puree, bay leaves, and 1 ½ cup water and bring to a boil, then reduce the heat to low and simmer, partially covered, 10 minutes.

4 Grind the almonds in a food processor until fine, then add them to the sauce. Add the brown sugar and chocolate and stir until the chocolate melts. Add the black beans and simmer, covered, 20 minutes, stirring regularly to prevent the sauce from sticking. Stir in the squash, season with salt and pepper, and warm through.

5 Meanwhile, cook the pancakes. Preheat the oven to 150°F. Add enough sunflower oil to lightly coat the bottom of a nonstick skillet and heat over medium heat. For each pancake, put ¼ cup of the batter in the pan and cook 2 to 3 minutes on each side until golden. Work in batches, if necessary, keeping the finished pancakes warm in the oven and adding more oil to the pan as needed.

6 Stir the lime zest into the crème fraîche, then peel, pit, and slice the avocado. Top the mole with the crème fraîche and avocado and

# CREAMY CHARD, PORCINI, AND PARMESAN PAPPARDELLE

**SERVES 4 TO 6**

1 ounce dried porcini mushrooms

13 ounces dried egg pappardelle

3 tablespoons olive oil

scant 3 cups sliced portobellini
    mushrooms

1 cup dry white wine

7 ounces rainbow chard, stems
    thinly sliced and leaves thickly
    sliced

scant 1 cup crème fraîche or sour
    cream

¾ cup finely grated Parmesan
    cheese

salt and freshly ground black pepper

1 Soak the porcini mushrooms in 1 cup plus 2 tablespoons boiling water 20 minutes or until soft. Strain, reserving the soaking liquid, and coarsely chop.

2 Cook the pappardelle in plenty of boiling salted water according to the package directions, then drain well.

3 Meanwhile, heat the olive oil in a large sauté pan over medium heat and fry the porcini, 4 minutes or until almost crisp, then add the portobellini mushrooms and fry 4 minutes longer, or until soft. Add the wine and bring to a boil, then cook over medium-high heat 5 minutes until it reduces by half. Add the reserved soaking liquid and cook 3 minutes or until it reduces.

4 Meanwhile, steam the chard 2 to 3 minutes until soft.

5 Stir the crème fraîche into the mushroom mixture, season well with salt and pepper, and then stir in half of the Parmesan. Add the drained pasta and chard and turn until coated. Sprinkle with the remaining Parmesan, season with salt and pepper, and serve.

# CHEESY POLENTA MASH WITH SHALLOT AND FENNEL CONFIT

**SERVES 4**

7 tablespoons olive oil

14 ounces shallots, peeled and
    quartered with the root ends
    intact or cut into 6 wedges, if large

1 eggplant, cut into bite-size pieces

1 large fennel bulb, cut into
    8 wedges

3 tablespoons apple juice

1 tablespoon balsamic vinegar

1 teaspoon light brown sugar

salt and freshly ground black pepper

**CHEESY POLENTA MASH**

1¼ cups instant polenta

3 tablespoons butter

½ cup finely grated Parmesan
    cheese

1 Heat the olive oil over medium heat in a deep sauté pan. Add the shallots in a single layer and sauté 7 minutes, stirring occasionally. Stir in the eggplant and fennel, then cover with a lid and cook over low heat 25 minutes, stirring occasionally to prevent the vegetables from sticking to the bottom of the pan.

2 Add the apple juice, balsamic vinegar, and brown sugar, then season with salt and pepper. Stir well and cook 10 minutes longer, or until the vegetables are very tender and the balsamic vinegar reduces.

3 Meanwhile, make the polenta. Heat 3½ cups water in a saucepan, sprinkle in the polenta, and bring to a boil, stirring. Reduce the heat to low and simmer, stirring frequently, 5 to 6 minutes until the polenta is smooth and creamy (it should be the same consistency as mashed potato). Stir in the butter and Parmesan and season with salt and pepper. Serve with the confit.

# ORIENTAL BLACK BEAN AND SHIITAKE RISOTTO

Chinese rice wine, fermented black beans, and shiitake mushrooms, with their rich, almost meaty, flavor, add an oriental twist to this classic creamy risotto. If desired, the risotto can be half cooked ahead of time, then, just before serving, reheat the stock and continue as instructed in step 4.

**SERVES 4**

3 tablespoons Chinese fermented black beans
2 tablespoons olive oil
2 onions, finely chopped
2-inch piece of ginger root, peeled and cut into matchsticks
7 ounces cremini mushrooms, halved
7 ounces shiitake mushrooms, sliced
1 ¾ cups arborio rice
²/₃ cup Chinese cooking wine or dry sherry
6 ½ cups vegetable stock, hot
2 tablespoons light soy sauce
¼ cup chopped cilantro leaves
2 tablespoons finely chopped chives
freshly ground black pepper

1 Soak the black beans in 3 tablespoons hot water 20 minutes, then drain and set aside.

2 Heat the olive oil in a large, heavy-bottomed saucepan over medium-low heat. Add the onions and cook, covered, 8 minutes, stirring occasionally, or until soft. Add the black beans, ginger, chestnut and shiitake mushrooms, and rice, then cook 2 minutes, stirring, until the rice is coated and glossy.

3 Add the Chinese wine and cook 3 minutes or until it is absorbed by the rice. Add a ladleful of hot stock, then stir continuously with a wooden spoon over a low heat until the rice absorbs the liquid.

4 Continue to add the stock, a ladleful at a time, simmering until all the stock is used and the rice is cooked and creamy but still retains a slight bite. Stir continuously to let the rice to cook evenly and to prevent it from sticking to the bottom of the pan. This will take about 25 minutes.

5 Stir in the soy sauce and half of the cilantro leaves and season with black pepper. Sprinkle with the chives and remaining cilantro leaves and serve.

# SUMMER PAELLA

This vegetarian version of the classic Spanish paella works brilliantly. The right type of rice—short-grain Calasparra—is essential, and the secret is to avoid stirring the rice during cooking so the bottom forms that desired golden crust. You can also serve this with a spoonful of Lemon and Garlic Mayonnaise (see page 138 ), if desired.

**SERVES 4**

⅓ cup blanched almonds
1 cup shelled fava beans
5 ounces asparagus tips
½ teaspoon saffron strands
3 tablespoons olive oil
2 onions, finely chopped
3 garlic cloves, chopped
1 large red bell pepper, seeded and diced
1 teaspoon smoked paprika
1 teaspoon turmeric
1¾ cups Calasparra rice
5 tablespoons dry sherry
4 cups vegetable stock
10 cherry tomatoes, halved
3 ounces small black olives
basil leaves, to serve
salt and freshly ground black pepper

1 Toast the almonds in a dry skillet over medium heat 3 to 4 minutes, stirring occasionally, until lightly browned. Then remove from the heat and set aside.

2 Blanch the fava beans in boiling water 3 minutes or until tender. Drain and refresh under cold running water, then gently squeeze the beans out of their outer skins into a bowl and set aside. Steam the asparagus 3 minutes or until just tender, then refresh under cold running water and set aside. Put the saffron and 1 tablespoon hot water in a small bowl and set aside to infuse.

3 Heat the olive oil over medium-low heat in a paella pan or large skillet with a lid. Fry the onions, stirring regularly, 5 minutes, then add the garlic and red pepper and fry, stirring occasionally, 3 minutes longer. Stir in the paprika, turmeric, and rice and stir 2 minutes or until coated in the oil.

4 Add the sherry and cook until it is absorbed by the rice. Stir in the saffron with its soaking liquid and stock. Bring to a boil, stir, then reduce the heat to its lowest setting. Simmer 20 minutes without stirring, or until the stock is absorbed. Remove the pan from the heat and top with the fava beans, cherry tomatoes, asparagus, and olives. Set aside, covered, 10 minutes to warm though.

5 Season with salt and pepper and serve topped with the almonds and basil.

# DAL WITH TOASTED ALMONDS

**SERVES 4 TO 6**

heaped 1 cup dried red lentils,
    rinsed
1 tablespoon sunflower oil
1 tablespoon mustard oil
1 large onion, finely chopped
3 garlic cloves, chopped
1-inch piece of ginger root, peeled
    and grated
2 teaspoons cumin seeds, ground
2 teaspoons mustard seeds, ground
12 curry leaves
2 teaspoons turmeric
5 tomatoes, peeled, seeded, and
    diced
3 small red chilies, slit open
    lengthwise
1 tablespoon tamarind paste
juice of 1 lime, plus wedges, to serve
2 tablespoons toasted slivered
    almonds
salt and freshly ground black pepper

1 Put the lentils in a saucepan and cover with 3½ cups water. Bring to a boil, then reduce the heat to low and simmer, partially covered, 25 to 30 minutes until the lentils are very tender and the water is absorbed.

2 Meanwhile, heat the sunflower and mustard oils in a large sauté pan over medium-low heat and sauté the onion 8 minutes or until soft and golden. Add the garlic, ginger, cumin and mustard seeds, and curry leaves and cook, stirring, 2 minutes.

3 Add the turmeric, tomatoes, and chilies, reduce the heat to low, and cook 3 minutes or until soft. Stir in the lentils, tamarind paste, and lime juice, cover, and warm through. Season with salt and pepper, top with the almonds and serve.

# RED ONION CHUTNEY

**SERVES 4**

2 tablespoons butter
2 tablespoons olive oil
2 cups thinly sliced red onions
¼ cup light brown sugar
scant ½ cup dry red wine
3 tablespoons balsamic vinegar
salt and freshly ground black pepper

1 Heat the butter and olive oil in a heavy-bottomed pan over medium-low heat and cook the onions, stirring occasionally, 15 minutes, partially covered, until soft. Add the muscovado sugar and cook over low heat, stirring often, 15 minutes longer, or until caramelized.

2 Increase the heat to medium and add the red wine and vinegar—take care as it will spit a bit. Cook 2 minutes, then reduce the heat to low. Simmer, partially covered, 10 to 15 minutes until reduced and thickened. Season with salt and pepper and let cool to room temperature before serving. Store in an airtight, sterilized jar in the refrigerator up to 2 months.

# BROCCOLINI WITH CHILI, LEMON, AND OLIVE OIL

**SERVES 4**

14 ounces broccolini
2 tablespoons butter
2 tablespoons lemon juice
finely grated zest of ½ lemon
1 medium red chili, seeded and
    finely chopped
salt

1  Boil the broccolini 2 minutes, then refresh under cold running
   water and drain well.
2  Heat the butter in a skillet over medium-low heat and add the
   lemon juice and zest and chili. Stir well, then add the broccolini.
   Season with salt and warm through, turning briefly, until coated,
   then serve.

# RICH ONION GRAVY

The perfect accompaniment to vegetarian savory pies and roasts. Cook the onions
slowly until they are soft and their natural sugars start to caramelize.

**SERVES 4**

2 tablespoons sunflower oil
2 onions, thinly sliced
2 tablespoons all-purpose flour
⅔ cup dry red wine
1½ cups vegetable stock
1 tablespoon vegetarian
    Worcestershire sauce
1 teaspoon Dijon mustard
salt and freshly ground black pepper

1  Heat the sunflower oil in a saucepan over medium-low heat and
   cook the onions 12 minutes, stirring regularly, until light golden.
   Add the flour and cook, stirring continuously, 1 minute longer.
2  Stir in the wine and bring to a boil, then reduce the heat to low and
   simmer 3 to 5 minutes or until the wine reduces by half.
3  Stir in the stock, Worcestershire sauce, and Dijon mustard and
   simmer 10 minutes or until thick. Season with salt and pepper
   and serve.

# GLAZED HONEY AND ROSEMARY BABY CARROTS

**SERVES 4**

1¼ pounds baby carrots, trimmed
2 tablespoons butter
1 tablespoon olive oil
1 large garlic clove, crushed
leaves from 2 rosemary sprigs,
    finely chopped
2 teaspoons wholegrain mustard
1 tablespoon honey

1  Boil the carrots 3 minutes or until almost tender, then drain well.
2  Heat the butter and olive oil in a sauté pan over medium-low
   heat. Add the garlic and rosemary and sauté 1 minute, then add
   the carrots, mustard, and honey. Cook over low heat, stirring
   continuously to prevent the honey from burning, 2 minutes or until
   the carrots are tender and coated in the sticky glaze, then serve.

# JEWELED PERSIAN RICE

**SERVES 4**

1¼ cups basmati rice
½ teaspoon salt, plus extra for
   seasoning
½ teaspoon saffron threads
2 tablespoons olive oil
1 onion, finely chopped
1 zucchini, diced
grated zest of 1 orange
1 teaspoon cumin seeds
1 teaspoon cinnamon
⅓ cup unsulfured dried apricots,
   chopped
⅓ cup blanched almonds, chopped
2 tablespoons plus 1 teaspoon
   butter
3 tablespoons dried barberries
freshly ground black pepper

1 If time allows, soak the rice for 1 hour, then drain and rinse under cold running water. Put the rice and salt in a saucepan and cover with water. Bring to a boil, then reduce the heat to low and simmer 4 minutes. Drain again and set aside. Clean the pan.

2 Put the saffron and ¼ cup hot water in a small bowl and set aside to infuse. Meanwhile, heat half of the olive oil in a skillet over medium-low heat and fry the onion 6 minutes, stirring occasionally, until soft. Add the zucchini and cook 3 minutes longer, then stir in the orange zest, cumin seeds, cinnamon, dried apricots, and almonds. Add the saffron and its soaking liquid, season with salt and pepper and mix well.

3 Heat the butter and remaining oil in the cleaned saucepan over medium-low heat. When it melts, add half of the rice and top with half of the vegetable mixture, then layer again with the rest of the rice and then the vegetable mixture. Using the handle of a wooden spoon, poke 5 holes into the rice and pour 1 teaspoon boiling water into each. Cover the pan with a tight-fitting lid and cook over low heat 10 to 15 minutes until the rice is tender and there is a light golden "crust" on the bottom. Sprinkle with the barberries and serve.

# PEAR CHUTNEY

**SERVES 4**

2 tablespoons olive oil
1 onion, finely chopped
1 garlic clove, finely chopped
1 teaspoon ground cumin
1 teaspoon ground coriander
½ teaspoon pumpkin pie spice
5 tablespoons red wine vinegar
¼ cup dark brown sugar
½ teaspoon salt
¼ cup unsulfured dried apricots,
   chopped
3 pears, peeled, cored, and chopped

1 Heat the olive oil in a heavy-bottomed saucepan over medium-low heat and fry the onion 6 minutes, stirring occasionally. Reduce the heat to low and fry, stirring occasionally, 6 minutes longer or until soft and golden in places.

2 Add the garlic and cook 1 minute, then stir in all of the remaining ingredients and bring to a boil. Reduce the heat to low and simmer, covered, 40 minutes until reduced and thickened. Stir occasionally to prevent the chutney from sticking. Let cool to room temperature before serving. Store in an airtight, sterilized jar in the refrigerator for up to a month.

# APPLE, BERRY, AND PLUM PUDDING WITH ROSE CREAM

Similar to the classic British summer pudding, this delicious version features a rich, dark, fruity sauce and sweet brioche, and is made in layers rather than in a bowl.

**SERVES 6**

3 apples, peeled, cored, and finely chopped

6 plums, halved, pitted, and chopped

1 cup plus 2 tablespoons freshly squeezed orange juice

scant ½ cup granulated sugar

1 teaspoon cinnamon

½ teaspoon freshly grated nutmeg

½ teaspoon ground ginger

2½ cups blackberries

14 ounces brioche loaf, sliced and crusts removed (optional)

**ROSE CREAM**

1 cup less 2 tablespoons heavy cream

2 tablespoons confectioners' sugar

1 teaspoon rosewater

1 Put the apples, plums, orange juice, sugar, cinnamon, nutmeg, and ginger in a saucepan and bring to a boil. Reduce the heat to low and simmer, partially covered, 8 minutes. Add the blackberries and simmer 4 to 8 minutes longer until the fruit is tender. Strain the cooking juice into a large measuring cup and set aside.

2 Arrange half of the brioche slices in a single layer in a 10- x 8-inch dish. Top with the cooked fruit and pour some of the strained juice over the top so the bread is ruby red.

3 Put a second layer of brioche on top of the fruit and pour enough of the cooking juice over to soak the bread, but do not let it become too soggy—you will still have some juice left over. Press a sheet of waxed paper over the top of the bread and weight down with a plate. Chill at least 3 hours, or overnight. Chill the reserved cooking juice until ready to serve.

4 To make the rose cream, whip the cream in a clean bowl until it forms soft peaks. Gradually beat in the confectioners' sugar and then stir in the rosewater. Cover and chill until required.

5 Cut the pudding into 6 portions and serve topped with a spoonful of the rose cream and drizzled with the reserved cooking juice.

# HOMEMADE CRÈME FRAÎCHE WITH CHERRY COMPOTE

Making your own crème fraîche is easy, but you do need to plan ahead. The rich, velvety, slightly sour cream will keep a couple of weeks in the refrigerator.

**SERVES 4**

1 cup plus 2 tablespoons heavy cream

4 teaspoons buttermilk

**CHERRY COMPOTE**

1 pound 8 ounces cherries

1/3 cup granulated sugar

2 tablespoons kirsch or brandy

2 teaspoons cornstarch

1 Gently warm the cream in a saucepan over medium-low heat to 105°F. Remove the pan from the heat and pour into a clean, glass jar. Stir in the buttermilk until well combined, then cover with plastic wrap or waxed paper and secure with a rubber band.

2 Put the jar in a warm, draft-free place and let thicken—this will take anything from 12 to 24 hours. Once thick, stir well, cover with a lid, and chill. The crème fraîche is ready to eat now but will continue to thicken. Store, covered, in the refrigerator up to 2 weeks. Serve chilled—it should have a slightly nutty, sour taste.

3 To make the cherry compote, put the cherries, sugar, and 2 tablespoons water in a saucepan and simmer 2 minutes, stirring to dissolve the sugar. Mix together the kirsch and cornstarch, then gradually stir the mixture into the cherries. Continue simmering 2 to 3 minutes longer, or until thickened. Serve with the crème fraîche.

# JASMINE TEA AND GINGER PEARS

These pears are poached in fragrant Jasmine tea that's flavored with aromatic ginger and star anise. Choose pears that are slightly underripe to prevent them from becoming too soft during poaching.

**SERVES 4**

4 slightly underripe pears

1 tablespoon lemon juice

3 Jasmine tea bags

8 thin slices of ginger root

1 cinnamon stick

1/4 cup granulated sugar

3 star anise

1 Peel and halve the pears and, using a melon baller or teaspoon, scoop out the cores. Coat in the lemon juice to prevent them from discoloring.

2 Bring 3 1/2 cups water to a boil in a large sauté pan. Reduce the heat to medium, add the Jasmine tea bags, and simmer 5 minutes, then remove the tea bags from the pan.

3 Add the pears, ginger, cinnamon, sugar, and star anise and simmer, partially covered, 15 to 20 minutes until tender. Using a slotted spoon, remove the pears from the pan. Increase the heat to medium-high and cook 2 to 3 minutes until the cooking liquid reduces and thickens. Remove and discard the spices. Serve 2 pear halves per person with the syrup spooned over the tops.

# SPICED CHOCOLATE MOUSSE WITH NUT BRITTLE

**SERVES 4**

3 ½ ounces dark chocolate, about 70% cocoa solids, broken into even-size pieces
2 extra-large eggs, separated
⅔ cup heavy cream
¼ cup granulated sugar
1 teaspoon ground allspice
½ teaspoon cinnamon

**NUT BRITTLE**

¾ cup granulated sugar
½ cup roasted salted peanuts, coarsely chopped
3 tablespoons butter

1 To make the nut brittle, line a baking sheet with baking parchment paper. Dissolve the sugar in a saucepan over low heat, stirring, until light golden. Stir in the peanuts and butter and, when the butter melts, pour the mixture onto the baking sheet. Let cool and harden, then break into pieces and set aside.

2 Put the chocolate in a heatproof bowl and rest it over a pan of gently simmering water, making sure the bottom of the bowl does not touch the water. Heat 4 to 5 minutes, stirring, until the chocolate melts, then set aside to cool slightly.

3 Beat the egg yolks and a large spoonful of the cream into the melted chocolate. In a large, clean bowl, beat the egg whites until they form soft peaks. Gradually beat in the sugar, allspice, and cinnamon until glossy soft peaks form.

4 Whip the cream until it forms soft peaks. Fold the chocolate mixture into the cream, followed by the egg white mixture. Spoon into four small ramekins or teacups and chill 1 hour, or until set. Serve each chocolate mousse with a piece of the nut brittle.

# LEMON POSSET WITH SESAME PHYLLO CRISPS

**SERVES 4**

1 ¾ cups heavy cream
¾ cup granulated sugar
¼ cup plus 2 teaspoons lemon juice
finely grated zest of 1 small lemon

**PHYLLO CRISPS**

1 phyllo pastry dough sheet, about 20 x 9 ½ inches
2 tablespoons butter, melted
2 tablespoons maple syrup
1 tablespoon sesame seeds

1 To make the phyllo crisps, preheat the oven to 400°F and line a baking sheet with baking parchment paper. Lay out the phyllo dough sheet on a work surface and cut it in half lengthwise, then cut each half into quarters. Brush each piece with melted butter and fold over lengthwise twice to make a ⅝-inch "stick". Brush the tops with the maple syrup and sprinkle with the sesame seeds. Bake 10 minutes or until crisp and light golden, then remove from the oven and let cool.

2 Put the cream and sugar in a saucepan and bring to a boil, stirring until the sugar dissolves. Reduce the heat to low and simmer 5 minutes, stirring occasionally, or until it is thick enough to coat the back of a spoon.

3 Remove the pan from the heat and stir in the lemon juice and zest. Pour the mixture into four espresso cups or small glasses. The possets can either be served warm, or chilled about 1 hour until set. Serve each lemon posset with 2 sesame phyllo crisps.

# RICE PUDDING WITH APRICOTS IN CARDAMOM SYRUP

**SERVES 4**

1 cup pudding rice

2⅔ cups milk

2 teaspoons cinnamon

1 teaspoon freshly grated nutmeg

6 tablespoons granulated sugar

finely grated zest of 1 large orange

3 tablespoons light cream

¼ cup slivered almonds, toasted

**APRICOTS IN CARDAMOM SYRUP**

2 cups dried unsulfured apricots

5 cardamom pods, lightly crushed

3 tablespoons honey

1 Put the apricots, cardamom, honey, and 1½ cups plus 2 tablespoons water in a saucepan and stir well. Bring to a boil, then reduce the heat to low and simmer, partially covered, 20 minutes or until the apricots are plump and tender and the sauce becomes syrupy. Remove the pan from the heat and set aside.

2 Meanwhile, put the rice and 2½ cups water in a heavy-bottomed saucepan. Bring to a boil, then reduce the heat to low and simmer, uncovered, 15 minutes or until the water is absorbed.

3 Stir in the milk, cinnamon, nutmeg, sugar, and orange zest and bring to a boil again. Reduce the heat to low and simmer, partially covered, 20 minutes, stirring regularly, or until the rice is cooked. Stir in the cream and gently heat through.

4 Divide the rice pudding into bowls, sprinkle with the almonds, and serve with the apricots and syrup.

# ZABAGLIONE WITH RHUBARB COMPOTE

**SERVES 4**

4 large egg yolks

¼ cup granulated sugar

5 tablespoons Marsala wine

**RHUBARB COMPOTE**

2½ cups thickly sliced rhubarb

½ teaspoon vanilla extract

¼ cup granulated sugar, plus extra as needed

1 To make the compote, put the rhubarb, vanilla extract, sugar, and 2 tablespoons water in a saucepan. Bring to a boil, then reduce the heat to low and simmer 7 minutes or until the rhubarb is very tender. Taste and add more sugar, if desired, remembering the zabaglione is sweet. Remove the pan from the heat and set aside.

2 Put the egg yolks and sugar in a heatproof bowl and rest it over a pan of simmering water, making sure the bottom of the bowl does not touch the water. Using an electric mixer, beat until the mixture is pale and the texture resembles heavy cream. Slowly add the Marsala wine and continue beating about 15 minutes or until the mixture almost triples in volume and become light, frothy, and creamy.

3 Divide half of the rhubarb compote into four glasses, then top with half of the zabaglione, followed by the rest of the compote and zabaglione. Swirl with a spoon to create a marbled effect, then serve immediately or chill until ready to eat.

# CHOCOLATE, GINGER, ALMOND, AND CHERRY SLAB

**SERVES 8**

⅓ cup blanched almonds

10 ounces dark chocolate, about 70% cocoa solids, broken into even-size pieces

1½ tablespoons preserved ginger in syrup, drained and coarsely chopped

¼ cup dried sour cherries

6 ounces white chocolate, broken into even-size pieces

1 Line a square 6-inch baking pan with plastic wrap and set aside. Toast the almonds in a dry skillet over medium heat 3 to 4 minutes, stirring occasionally, until light brown, then set aside.

2 Put the dark chocolate in a heatproof bowl and rest it over a pan of gently simmering water, making sure the bottom of the bowl does not touch the water. Heat 4 to 5 minutes, stirring, until the chocolate melts. Carefully remove the bowl from the heat and stir in the ginger, cherries, and almonds. Pour the mixture into the prepared pan and spread into an even layer.

3 Melt the white chocolate, following the same directions as in step 2 for the dark chocolate. Dot spoonfuls of the melted white chocolate on top of the dark chocolate and, using a skewer, swirl the chocolates together to create a marbled pattern.

4 Put the chocolate slab in the refrigerator and chill 1 hour, or until set. Break into large chunks and store in an airtight container in the refrigerator until ready to eat.

# ESPRESSO POTS WITH CARAMELIZED COFFEE SAUCE

**SERVES 6**

1 cup plus 2 tablespoons heavy cream

1 cup plus 2 tablespoons milk

1 teaspoon vanilla extract

2 tablespoons brewed espresso coffee

3 large eggs

scant ⅓ cup granulated sugar

CARAMELIZED COFFEE SAUCE

1 cup granulated sugar

scant ½ cup brewed espresso coffee

2 tablespoons butter

1 Preheat the oven to 315°F. To make the caramelized coffee sauce, put the sugar in a heavy-bottomed saucepan over medium heat, stirring occasionally, 5 minutes or until it melts and turns a rich golden brown. Remove the pan from the heat and stir in the coffee, taking care as it will froth up—it is a good idea to wear an oven mitt. Return the pan to low heat, stir until combined and smooth, then stir in the butter. Remove the pan from the heat and set aside.

2 Gently heat the cream, milk, vanilla extract, and coffee in a separate saucepan over medium-low heat until just below a boil, then remove from the heat and let cool slightly.

3 Meanwhile, whisk together the eggs and sugar, then stir in the cream mixture. Divide into six ⅔-cup ramekins or ovenproof glasses and put them in a baking dish. Add enough water to the dish to come halfway up the sides of the ramekins and bake 25 minutes or until just set (they will still be very wobbly). Carefully remove the ramekins from the dish, let the custards cool at room temperature 15 minutes, and then chill until set.

4 Pour some of the caramelized coffee sauce over each espresso pot and serve.

More than with any other method of cooking, baking cleverly lets you know when foods are ready by releasing a tantalizing aroma that's impossible to ignore. From colorful vegetable tarts and golden pies to sumptuous cakes and roasted fruits, these recipes are full of stunning flavors.

# BAKE

Roasted Balsamic Pears, page 222

# INDIAN-STYLE PANZANELLA

This dish incorporates all the elements associated with the rustic Italian bread salad but comes with an Indian twist. Paneer is a semihard, mild-tasting Indian cheese and is sold in blocks in Asian food stores or supermarkets.

**SERVES 4**

6 tablespoons balti or other curry paste
2 tablespoons sunflower oil, plus extra for greasing and deep-frying
10 ounces paneer cheese, cut into 12 slices
1 cup cooked chickpeas
2 small naan breads, split open
9 ounces cherry tomatoes, halved
1 small cucumber, quartered lengthwise, seeded, and cut into small chunks
1 small red onion, sliced into thin rings
1 small fennel bulb, thinly sliced
juice of 1 lime
4 uncooked poppadoms
½ cup plain yogurt
1 garlic clove, crushed
1 teaspoon cumin seeds
salt and freshly ground black pepper
mint leaves, to serve

1 Mix together the curry paste and sunflower oil in a shallow dish. Add the paneer and turn to coat in the mixture, then set aside to marinate 1 hour.

2 Preheat the oven to 350°F and lightly grease a large baking sheet with oil. Using a slotted spoon, remove the paneer from the marinade and put it on the baking sheet. Add the chickpeas to the marinade and turn until coated, then transfer to the baking sheet. Roast the paneer and chickpeas 20 to 25 minutes, turning occasionally, until the paneer is golden and the chickpeas are slightly crisp.

3 Meanwhile, put the naan bread on an ungreased baking sheet and bake 5 to 8 minutes until crisp. Let cool, then break into bite-size pieces.

4 Put the tomatoes, cucumber, onion, and fennel in a bowl, add half the lime juice, and season with salt and pepper, then toss well and set aside.

5 Heat 2 inches sunflower oil in a wide saucepan over medium-high heat until it reaches 375°F. A cube of bread will turn golden in 20 seconds when dropped into the oil. Cook the poppadoms, one at a time, 2 to 3 seconds each, holding it under the oil with a spatula until puffed up and crisp. Drain on paper towels.

6 Mix together the yogurt, garlic, and remaining lime juice in a bowl. Season with salt and pepper, then sprinkle with the cumin seeds.

7 Put 1 poppadom on each of four plates and top with the tomato salad. Scatter the chickpeas and naan bread over the salad, then top with the paneer and a large spoonful of the yogurt mixture. Sprinkle with a few mint leaves and serve.

# LINGUINE BAKED IN PAPER

The paper packages keep in all the lovely juices and the flavor of the herbs, wine, tomatoes, and garlic, which infuse the pasta during baking. There's no need to remove the paper after cooking, as it adds to the stylish presentation.

**SERVES 4**

13½ ounces linguine
2 tablespoons olive oil
2 large garlic cloves, finely chopped
1 long red chili, seeded and finely chopped
1 cup less 2 tablespoons dry white wine
1 pound cherry tomatoes
3 tablespoons small capers, drained and rinsed
3 tablespoons chopped flat-leaf parsley leaves
salt and freshly ground black pepper
Parmesan cheese shavings, to serve

1 Cook the pasta in plenty of boiling salted water until almost cooked, about 10 minutes, then drain, reserving 2 tablespoons of the cooking water.

2 Meanwhile, heat the olive oil in a skillet and fry the garlic and chili 1 minute, stirring occasionally. Add the wine and bring to a boil, then reduce the heat slightly and cook 3 to 5 minutes until the wine reduces by about one-third and the alcohol evaporates.

3 Preheat the oven to 350°F. Add the tomatoes and capers to the skillet and cook, stirring occasionally, 3 minutes or until slightly soft. Add the pasta, reserved cooking water, and parsley. Remove the pan from the heat and stir until the pasta is coated in the sauce.

4 Put a large sheet of baking parchment paper in each of four bowls and divide the pasta into them. Gather up the edges of the paper and tie with kitchen string, then put the packages on a baking sheet and bake 15 minutes. To serve, return the packages to the bowls and open carefully. Sprinkle with Parmesan, season with black pepper, and serve.

# ITALIAN BAKED LEMONS WITH MOZZARELLA

**SERVES 4**

3 large lemons

12 large basil leaves

3 x 4½-ounce mozzarella balls, drained, patted dry, and cut into 12 slices

12 sun-blush tomatoes in oil, drained

salt and freshly ground black pepper

**1** Slice off and discard the ends of the lemons, then cut each one into 4 slices, each about ½ inch thick. Using a sharp knife, cut around and remove the flesh (saving it for another use) so you are left with 12 rings of lemon peel. Preheat the oven to 350°F and line a large baking sheet with baking parchment paper.

**2** Put each lemon ring on each basil leaf and arrange on the baking sheet. Press 1 slice of mozzarella into each ring and top with 1 sun-blush tomato. Bake 8 to 10 minutes until the mozzarella melts slightly and is heated through—it shouldn't be allowed to get too soft or it will seep out of its shell. Season with salt and pepper and serve warm.

# ROASTED ROOT VEGETABLE SOUP

Roasting the vegetables enhances their natural sweetness, adding a depth of flavor to this hearty soup. Feel free to adapt the root vegetables depending on what you have to hand and what is in season.

**SERVES 4 TO 6**

1 small winter squash, such as butternut, kabocha, or pumpkin, peeled, seeded, and cut into bite-size chunks

2 parsnips, cut into ½-inch slices

2 carrots, cut into ½ in slices

2 onions, peeled and quartered

1 rutabaga, peeled and cut into bite-size chunks

1 garlic bulb, top trimmed

3 tablespoons olive oil

4 long rosemary sprigs

a few thyme sprigs

6½ cups vegetable stock

2 bay leaves

salt and freshly ground black pepper

sour cream, to serve

**1** Preheat the oven to 400°F. Put the squash, parsnips, carrots, onions, rutabaga, and garlic in a large bowl. Drizzle the olive oil over them, season with salt and pepper, and then toss until evenly coated. Spread the vegetables out in a single layer in two baking trays and add the rosemary and thyme. Bake 25 minutes, then remove the garlic bulb and herbs and return the remaining vegetables to the oven, swapping the trays around. Bake 20 to 25 minutes longer until tender.

**2** Squeeze the soft garlic out of each clove and put it in a large saucepan. Add the roasted vegetables, stock, and bay leaves and bring to a boil over high heat. Reduce the heat to low and simmer 10 to 15 minutes until the vegetables are very tender. Remove and discard the bay leaves, then blend the soup until smooth and thick, adding more stock if necessary.

**3** Reheat the soup, if necessary, taste and season again with salt and pepper, if desired. Divide into bowls, top with a swirl of sour cream, and serve.

# ROASTED SWEET POTATO AND SMOKED TOFU SALAD

**SERVES 4**

¼ cup black bean sauce

2 tablespoons light soy sauce

1 teaspoon sunflower oil, plus extra
   for greasing

3 teaspoons sesame oil

8 ounces smoked tofu, cut into
   bite-size cubes

2 sweet potatoes, peeled and cut
   into bite-size cubes

2 tablespoons pumpkin seeds

4 romaine lettuce leaves, shredded

1½ cups shredded red cabbage

½ red onion, finely chopped

3 tablespoons olive oil

2 tablespoons lemon juice

1 handful of broccoli sprouts,
   to serve

salt and freshly ground black pepper

1 Mix together the black bean sauce, soy sauce, sunflower oil, and 1 teaspoon of the sesame oil in a shallow dish. Add the tofu, turn to coat in the marinade, then set aside to marinate at least 30 minutes.

2 Preheat the oven to 375°F and lightly grease two baking sheets with sunflower oil. Put the tofu on one of the baking sheets and bake 20 to 25 minutes, turning once, until golden all over. At the same time, put the sweet potato on the other baking sheet, turn to coat in the oil and season with salt and pepper. Roast 20 to 25 minutes, turning once, until tender and golden.

3 Meanwhile, toast the pumpkin seeds in a dry skillet over medium heat 3 to 4 minutes, stirring occasionally, until light brown, then remove from the heat and set aside.

4 Divide the lettuce, cabbage, and red onion into four large, shallow bowls. Mix together the olive oil, lemon juice, and remaining sesame oil and season with salt and pepper. Drizzle the dressing over the salad and top with the roasted sweet potatoes and tofu. Sprinkle with the toasted pumpkin seeds and broccoli sprouts, then serve.

# TIAN OF SUMMER VEGETABLES

**SERVES 4**

6 tablespoons olive oil, plus extra for
   drizzling

1 eggplant, cut into ¼-inch slices

1 large onion, thinly sliced

2 garlic cloves, chopped

2 red bell peppers, seeded and sliced

1 large handful of basil leaves

9 ounces mozzarella balls, drained
   and sliced

2 zucchini, sliced diagonally

2 tomatoes, sliced

4 teaspoons butter

6 tablespoons fresh bread crumbs

1 red chili, seeded and chopped

¼ cup grated Parmesan cheese

salt and freshly ground black pepper

1 Heat 2 tablespoons of the olive oil in a large skillet. Fry half of the eggplant 4 minutes on each side until soft and slightly golden. Remove from the pan with a slotted spoon and arrange in a single layer in a 10½- x 8-inch baking dish. Repeat with the remaining eggplant, adding a little more oil, if necessary. Add the onion to the pan and fry, stirring occasionally, 8 minutes or until soft. Add the garlic and cook 2 minutes longer.

2 Preheat the oven to 400°F. Top the eggplant with a layer of peppers, half of the basil, and half of the mozzarella. Spread the onion and garlic over the cheese and arrange the zucchini in an even layer on top. Layer again with the remaining basil and mozzarella, then with the tomatoes. Drizzle with olive oil, season with salt and pepper, and bake 35 to 45 minutes until the vegetables are cooked and the mozzarella is bubbling.

3 Meanwhile, melt the butter in a skillet, then fry the bread crumbs 5 minutes or until light golden. Add the chili and cook 1 minute, then remove from the heat and stir in the Parmesan. Sprinkle the mixture over the tian and serve.

# BLACK OLIVE FARINATA WITH SPINACH TZATZIKI

Farinata is a type of Italian pancake made with chickpea flour. Variations exist in North Africa and South America.

**SERVES 4**

heaped 1⅓ cups chickpea flour
½ teaspoon salt
1 extra-large egg, lightly beaten
5 tablespoons olive oil
⅓ cup pitted black olives, halved
heaped 1 tablespoon chopped
    rosemary
1 red onion, thinly sliced
1 red chili, seeded and thinly sliced
salt and freshly ground black pepper

**SPINACH TZATZIKI**

⅔ cup plain yogurt
1 small garlic clove, chopped
9 ounces spinach leaves, tough
    stems removed
squeeze of lemon juice

1 Put the chickpea flour and salt in a bowl and make a well in the middle. Add the egg, 2 tablespoons of the olive oil, 1¾ cups lukewarm water. Using a wooden spoon, gradually draw the flour into the wet ingredients and stir to make a thick, smooth batter, then cover and let rest 1 hour.

2 Meanwhile, make the spinach tzatziki. Mix together the yogurt, garlic, and ¼ cup water. Steam the spinach 2 minutes, or until it wilts, then drain well and press the spinach with the back of a wooden spoon to squeeze out any excess water. Unravel the spinach and mix it into the yogurt mixture. Stir in a squeeze of lemon juice, season with salt and pepper, and chill until needed.

3 Preheat the oven to 425°F. Pour the remaining oil into a 13- x 9-inch baking tray and heat in the oven 2 to 3 minutes until very hot, then carefully remove the tray from the oven. While the oil is heating, skim any froth off the top of the farinata batter and stir well.

4 Carefully pour the batter into the baking tray and sprinkle the olives, rosemary, onion, and chili over the top and bake 15 to 20 minutes until set and golden. Cut into squares and serve warm with the tzatziki.

# BAKED EGGS IN PHYLLO WITH TOMATO PICKLE AND GARLIC MUSHROOMS

Phyllo pastry dough makes simple and pretty individual pastry shells. When using phyllo, it's important not to let it dry out, so keep the unused dough covered with a clean, slightly damp dish towel while you work.

**SERVES 4**
5 tablespoons butter, melted
4 large sheets phyllo pastry dough
8 large eggs

**TOMATO PICKLE**
2 tbsp olive oil
1 onion, finely chopped
5 tomatoes, seeded and chopped
1 teaspoon Dijon mustard
¼ cup white wine vinegar
2 tablespoons light brown sugar
salt and freshly ground black pepper

**GARLIC MUSHROOMS**
2 tablespoons olive oil
butter, melted
3½ cups sliced cremini mushrooms
3 garlic cloves, finely chopped
1 tablespoon chopped parsley
   leaves

1 First make the tomato pickle. Heat the olive oil in a pan over medium-low heat and fry the onion 8 minutes, stirring occasionally, until soft. Add the tomatoes, mustard, vinegar, and brown sugar and season with salt and pepper. Bring to a boil, then reduce the heat to low and simmer, partially covered, 10 to 15 minutes until thicker. Transfer to a serving bowl.

2 Preheat the oven to 400°F and brush 8 holes of a deep muffin pan with a little of the melted butter. Lay the phyllo pastry sheets on top of one another and cut them in half crosswise, then cut each half into 4 squares. Take one square and brush a little butter between each layer of phyllo dough, then press it into a muffin hole to make a "basket" shape. Repeat with the remaining phyllo dough to make 8 baskets, then brush the overhanging dough (but not the inside) with a little more butter. Break 1 egg into each phyllo basket, season with salt and pepper, and bake 12 to 15 minutes until the eggs are just set and the pastry is golden.

3 While the eggs are baking, make the garlic mushrooms. Put the olive oil and butter into a skillet and fry the mushrooms 5 minutes or until tender. Add the garlic, season with salt and pepper, and fry 2 minutes longer, then sprinkle with the parsley. Top the eggs with the mushrooms and serve with the tomato pickle.

# CAULIFLOWER AND CHEESE CUSTARDS WITH ROASTED TOMATOES

Cheese and cauliflower are a classic combination, and here they are turned into light, savory puddings. Roasting intensifies the flavor of the tomatoes and the combination of brown sugar, balsamic vinegar, and harissa gives them a slightly caramelized, spicy stickiness.

**SERVES 4**

1 small cauliflower, cut into small florets
7 tablespoons milk
4 large eggs
¼ cup crème fraîche or sour cream
heaped 1 cup grated sharp cheddar cheese
salt and freshly ground black pepper
8 thick slices of toasted crusty bread, to serve

**ROASTED TOMATOES**

2 tablespoons olive oil, plus extra for greasing
2 tablespoons balsamic vinegar
½ to 1 teaspoon harissa paste, to taste
12 tomatoes, halved lengthwise
1 teaspoon dark brown sugar
1 heaped teaspoon coriander seeds, crushed

1 To make the roasted tomatoes, preheat the oven to 350°F, and line a baking tray with foil and grease lightly. Mix together the olive oil, balsamic vinegar, and harissa in a shallow dish and season with salt and pepper. Add the tomatoes and turn until coated, then arrange them, cut-sides up, on the baking tray. Sprinkle with the brown sugar and coriander seeds and bake 50 to 55 minutes until softened and slightly caramelized.

2 Meanwhile, steam the cauliflower 5 minutes or until tender. Transfer to a blender, add the milk and puree until smooth. In a mixing bowl, whisk together the eggs and crème fraîche, then stir in the cheddar and cauliflower puree. Season with salt and pepper, then divide the mixture into four ¾-cup ramekins arranged on a baking tray.

3 After the tomatoes have been cooking 30 minutes, put the baking tray in the oven and bake the custards alongside the tomatoes 20 to 25 minutes until set and risen.

4 Serve the cauliflower custards with the roasted tomatoes and toasted bread.

# CHAR SUI TEMPEH WITH CHINESE PANCAKES

Tempeh is made from fermented soybeans and has a firm texture and nutty, mushroomy flavor. Like tofu, which is also made from soybeans, it benefits from marinating and readily takes on the flavor of stronger ingredients.

**SERVES 4**

12 ounces tempeh
5 tablespoons hoisin sauce
3 tablespoons light soy sauce
1 teaspoon sunflower oil
3 tablespoons honey
1 teaspoon Chinese five-spice
  powder
8 Chinese pancakes
1 small cucumber, seeded and cut
  into strips
3 scallions, thinly sliced lengthwise
  into strips
1 red chili, seeded and thinly sliced
8 large basil leaves

1 Steam the tempeh 5 minutes until soft—this also helps to remove any trace of bitterness.

2 Mix together the hoisin sauce, soy sauce, sunflower oil, honey, and Chinese five-spice in a shallow dish. Add the tempeh, turn to coat in the marinade, and then let marinate 1 hour. Meanwhile, preheat the oven to 400°F.

3 Loosely wrap the tempeh in foil and put it in a roasting pan, reserving any leftover marinade. Bake 15 minutes, then remove the foil package from the oven. Meanwhile, preheat the broiler to medium-high.

4 Carefully remove the tempeh from the oven and unwrap. Pour off and reserve any cooking juices in the foil and return the tempeh to the roasting pan. Spoon some of the marinade over the tempeh and broil 5 minutes or until golden and glossy, turning halfway and spooning more of the marinade over the tempeh. Slice the tempeh into long strips. Combine any leftover marinade with the reserved cooking juices.

5 Meanwhile, wrap the Chinese pancakes in foil and heat them 3 to 4 minutes in the still-warm oven. Put the pancakes on plates and divide the tempeh over them. Top each one with a spoonful of the marinade, then the cucumber, scallions, chili, and basil. Roll up the pancakes or serve flat.

# MUSHROOM AND CASHEW PIES WITH RED ONION CHUTNEY

There's something very appealing about an individual savory pie. They make a hearty weekend lunch served with Rich Onion Gravy (see page 179), and their portable size means they're ideal for picnics, too.

**SERVES 4**

¾ ounce dried porcini mushrooms
2 tablespoons olive oil
2 onions, finely chopped
3 garlic cloves, finely chopped
3½ cups coarsely chopped cremini mushrooms
2 teaspoons dried thyme
3 tablespoons sherry
1 tablespoon dark soy sauce
heaped 1 cup broken cashew nuts
1½ cups fresh bread crumbs
½ cup very finely ground blanched almonds
beaten egg, for glazing
salt and freshly ground black pepper
1 recipe quantity Red Onion Chutney (see page 178), to serve

**PASTRY DOUGH**

1⅔ cups all-purpose flour, plus extra for rolling out the dough
½ teaspoon salt
¼ cup cold butter, diced, plus extra for greasing
1 egg yolk

1 First make the pastry dough. Sift the flour and salt into a bowl. Rub in the butter with your fingertips until the mixture resembles fine bread crumbs. Add the egg yolk and a little cold water, if necessary, and mix to combine; press the dough together to make a smooth ball, wrap in plastic wrap, and chill 30 minutes.

2 Meanwhile, put the porcini mushrooms in a small heatproof bowl and just cover with boiling water, then let soak 20 minutes. Strain the mushrooms, reserving 3 tablespoons of the soaking liquid, then roughly chop.

3 Heat the olive oil over medium-low heat and fry the onions, stirring occasionally, 15 to 20 minutes, partially covered, until golden and very soft. Add the garlic, porcini and chestnut mushrooms, and thyme and fry, uncovered, 5 minutes, stirring occasionally. Add the sherry, soy sauce, and reserved mushroom liquid and simmer 2 minutes or until the liquid reduces by half.

4 Finely grind the cashews in a food processor and transfer to a large mixing bowl. Stir in the bread crumbs and almonds. Put the mushroom mixture in the food processor and process to a smooth paste, then add to the cashews. Season with salt and pepper and stir until well combined and the mixture has the consistency of a firm pâté.

5 Preheat the oven to 400°F. Grease four ⅔-cup dariole molds. Roll out the dough on a lightly floured work surface and cut out 4 circles to line the molds, then gathering up the trimmings. Put 1 circle in each mold and press it from the bottom upward to get rid of any air bubbles and shape it into a pie shell. Leave ¾-inch of the dough overhanging the top of the molds.

6 Fill the pie shells nearly to the top with the mushroom mixture. Reroll the dough trimmings and cut out 4 circles to fit as lids on top of the molds. Wet the edge of each pie shell with water and press the lid on the top, pinching with your fingers to seal. Trim off any excess dough.

7 Brush the tops with egg, put the pies on a baking sheet, and bake 35 to 40 minutes until golden. Let rest 2 to 3 minutes before loosening the pies with a knife and carefully turning them out. Serve hot with chutney.

# RED ONION, BEET. AND GOAT CHEESE TART

The walnut pastry in this tart complements the earthy quality of the beets, as well as the slight sweetness of the red onions and goat cheese. If time allows, boil or roast the beet or, alternatively, buy cooked beets—but make sure to choose ones in natural juice rather than pickled in vinegar.

**SERVES 4 TO 6**

1 tablespoon olive oil

2 tablespoons unsalted butter, plus extra for greasing

1 pound 8 ounces red onions, thinly sliced

5 thyme sprigs, plus extra to serve

3 tablespoons balsamic vinegar

14 ounces cooked baby beets, halved lengthwise

1 tablespoon honey

6 ounces goat cheese, crumbled

salt and freshly ground black pepper

**WALNUT PASTRY DOUGH**

½ cup walnuts

1¼ cups all-purpose flour, sifted, plus extra for rolling the dough

6 tablespoons cold butter, diced

1 egg, separated

1 To make the pastry dough, toast the walnuts in a dry skillet over medium heat 4 to 5 minutes, turning occasionally, until light golden, then chop finely and set aside. Put the flour, a generous pinch of salt, and butter in a food processor and pulse until it resembles fine bread crumbs. Add the walnuts, egg yolk, and 2 to 3 tablespoons cold water and continue to pulse until the mixture forms a ball of dough. Remove the dough from the food processor, wrap in plastic wrap, and chill 30 minutes.

2 Meanwhile, heat the oil and butter in a large sauté pan and fry the onions over low heat, partially covered, 20 minutes, stirring occasionally, until soft but not colored. Add the thyme and balsamic vinegar and cook 5 minutes longer until the vinegar is absorbed. Add the beets and honey and stir until glossy, then season with salt and pepper and set aside.

3 Meanwhile, preheat the oven to 350°F and lightly grease a 9½-inch loose-bottomed tart pan with butter. Roll out the dough on a lightly floured work surface and gently press it into the prepared pan. Prick the tart shell a few times with a fork, then line it with baking parchment paper and fill with baking beans. Bake 20 minutes until almost baked, then remove the beans and paper and bake 15 minutes until light brown and baked through.

4 Brush the tart shell with beaten egg white and fill with the onion and beet mixture. Arrange the goat cheese on top and bake 15 minutes or until the cheese has browned in places. Decorate with a few thyme sprigs and serve.

# BAKED TOMATO RISOTTO WITH WINTER PESTO AND PARMESAN–WALNUT CRISPS

This risotto goes against the grain: it's baked in the oven rather than cooked on the stovetop, and conveniently only needs to be stirred once. Topped with a spoonful of the aromatic winter herb pesto and a feather-light Parmesan crisps, it's comfort food at its most perfect.

**SERVES 4**

½ cup chopped walnuts, halved

heaped ¼ cup grated Parmesan cheese, plus extra shaved, to serve

2 tablespoons olive oil

2 tablespoons butter

2 onions, finely chopped

3 garlic cloves, finely chopped

1½ cups risotto rice

¾ cup dry red wine

2 cups plus 2 tablespoons hot vegetable stock

2 cups plus 2 tablespoons pureed tomatoes

heaped 1 teaspoon sun-dried tomato paste

salt and freshly ground black pepper

**WINTER PESTO**

½ ounce mixed herbs, including sage, rosemary, and thyme

1 garlic clove

6 tablespoons olive oil

heaped ¼ cup grated Parmesan cheese

1 Preheat the oven to 350°F. Put the walnuts on a baking sheet and bake 3 to 4 minutes until lightly toasted. Remove from the oven and let cool slightly, then finely chop half of the walnuts and set the rest aside.

2 To make the Parmesan crisps, line the baking sheet with baking parchment paper. Sprinkle 1 tablespoon of the Parmesan into a mound on the baking sheet, then sprinkle one-quarter of the chopped walnuts over it. Tidy the edges slightly to make a circle about 1½ inches in diameter, then repeat to make 3 more circles, spacing them out by at least 2 inches as they tend to spread during cooking. Bake 10 minutes or until golden and crisp. Let cool for a few minutes before lifting them off the baking sheet with a metal spatula and set aside.

3 Heat the olive oil and half of the butter in a large ovenproof saucepan. Fry the onions, partially covered, 10 minutes, stirring occasionally, until soft. Add the garlic and risotto rice and cook, stirring, 3 minutes longer, or until the rice is glossy and coated in the oil. Add the wine and cook, stirring, until it is absorbed by the rice. Add the stock, tomato puree, and sun-dried tomato paste and season with salt and pepper. Stir until well combined.

4 Cover the risotto with a tight-fitting, ovenproof lid and bake 40 minutes, stirring once halfway through. Remove from the oven, stir in the remaining butter, and set aside, covered, 5 minutes.

5 Meanwhile, make the pesto. Put the remaining walnuts in a food processor and add the herbs and garlic. Process until coarsely chopped, then add the olive oil and process again to make a coarse paste. Transfer the mixture to a bowl and stir in the Parmesan, then season with salt and pepper.

6 Stir the risotto and divide it into four large, shallow bowls. Top with a good spoonful of the pesto and shaved Parmesan and serve with the Parmesan crisps.

# HERB RICOTTA FLAN WITH ROASTED TOMATO PESTO

Ricotta makes a light, summery flan but make sure you buy good-quality cheese. The roasted tomato pesto is the perfect accompaniment, adding both color and intense flavor. Serve the flan cut into wedges with boiled new potatoes and a watercress salad.

**SERVES 6**

3 cups ricotta cheese

1 cup finely grated Parmesan cheese

3 extra-large eggs, separated

1/4 cup torn basil leaves, plus whole leaves to garnish

1/4 cup oregano leaves, plus extra to garnish

1 teaspoon salt, plus extra for seasoning

freshly ground black pepper

**ROASTED TOMATO PESTO**

1/4 cup pine nuts

14 ounces cherry tomatoes

5 1/2 tablespoons olive oil, plus extra for greasing

1/2 cup coarsely chopped drained sun-blush tomatoes in oil

1 garlic clove

1 Preheat the oven to 350°F and lightly grease an 8-inch loose-bottomed pan with a little of the olive oil. Put the ricotta, Parmesan, and egg yolks in a food processor and blend until smooth and creamy. Transfer to a large mixing bowl and stir in the basil, oregano, salt and season with plenty of pepper.

2 Beat the egg whites in a separate bowl until they form stiff peaks. Using a metal spoon, gently fold the egg whites into the ricotta mixture. Transfer the batter to the pan and smooth the top with a metal spatula. Bake on the lower rack of the oven 30 minutes.

3 Meanwhile, put the cherry tomatoes for the pesto in a roasting pan with 2 tablespoons of the oil, season with salt and pepper, and toss well. After the flan has been baking 30 minutes, put the tomatoes in the top half of the oven above the flan and bake both 30 minutes longer, or until the flan is set and the top is light golden and the tomatoes are soft. Remove both from the oven. Let the flan cool slightly, then run a knife around the edge of the flan before removing from the pan.

4 To make the pesto, toast the pine nuts in a dry skillet and over medium heat 3 to 4 minutes, stirring occasionally, until lightly browned. Watch carefully so they do not burn. Remove from the heat and put half of them in a food processor. Add the roasted tomatoes, olive oil, sun-blush tomatoes and garlic and process to a coarse paste, then season with salt and pepper.

5 Cut the flan into wedges and serve with the roasted tomato pesto, topped with the remaining basil, oregano, and pine nuts.

# CHESTNUT, STILTON, AND ALE PUFF PASTRY PIE

This is a hearty savory pie for a cold winter's day. The Stilton cheese melts into the ale sauce, enriching it and helping create a thick gravy for the vegetable and chestnut filling.

**SERVES 4**

1 tablespoon olive oil
2 onions, coarsely chopped
1 celery stick, sliced
3 cups halved and thickly sliced
   large, flat mushrooms
2 parsnips, peeled and cut into
   bite-size chunks
8 ounces baby carrots, trimmed
   (or 3 regular carrots, sliced)
1 cup thickly sliced cooked
   chestnuts
1 teaspoon dried thyme
1 cup less 2 tablespoons light ale
scant ½ cup vegetable stock
2 teaspoons vegetarian
   Worcestershire sauce
2 tablespoons all-purpose flour, plus
   extra for rolling the dough
heaped ½ cup coarsely chopped
   Stilton cheese with the rind
   removed
10 ounces puff pastry dough
all-purpose flour, for rolling the
   dough
1 egg, lightly beaten
salt and freshly ground black pepper

1 Preheat the oven to 400°F. Heat the oil in a large pan over medium-low heat and fry the onions, partially covered, 10 minutes, stirring occasionally, until soft and golden. Add the celery, mushrooms, parsnips, and carrots and sauté 10 minutes, stirring often. Stir in the chestnuts and thyme.

2 Add the ale and bring to a boil, then reduce the heat to medium-low and cook 3 to 5 minutes until the liquid reduces by half. Add the stock and Worcestershire sauce and return to a simmer. Mix together the flour and 1 tablespoon water and stir this mixture into the vegetables. Cook, stirring, 5 to 10 minutes until the gravy reduces and thickens. Add the Stilton, stir until combined, and season to taste with salt and pepper.

3 Transfer the mixture to a 10½ x 8-inch baking dish. Roll out the puff pastry dough on a lightly floured surface so it is large enough to cover the dish. Wet the edge of the dish with water and lay the dough on top of the filling, leaving a slight overhang. Trim off the excess dough and use the back of a fork to seal the edges. Brush the top of the pie with egg and gently prick it in a few places with a fork. Bake 35 to 40 minutes until risen and golden. Serve hot.

# JERUSALEM ARTICHOKE, CELERY ROOT, AND BLUE CHEESE TARTLETS

These individual tarts have a delicious crisp and buttery tart shell. Their free-form shape lends a rustic charm, which suits the earthy flavor of the root vegetable filling, but for a more refined look you can use small individual fluted tart pans.

**MAKES 6**

1 large Jerusalem artichoke, unpeeled and thinly sliced lengthwise, outer slices discarded
1 tablespoon olive oil, plus extra for greasing
3 cups peeled celery root cut into bite-size pieces
3 tablespoons plus 1 teaspoon butter
7 tablespoons milk
2 tablespoons chopped flat-leaf parsley leaves
½ cup crumbled dolcelatte or Cashel Blue cheese
salt and freshly ground black pepper
1 recipe quantity Rosemary and Sea Salt Crushed Potatoes (see page 220), to serve

**PASTRY DOUGH**

7 tablespoons chilled butter, diced, plus extra for greasing
heaped ¾ cup all-purpose flour, sifted, plus extra for rolling the dough
¼ cup sour cream

1 To make the pastry dough, put the butter and flour in a food processor and pulse until it resembles fine bread crumbs. Add the sour cream and continue to pulse until the dough starts to come together. Remove the dough from the food processor, shape into a ball, wrap in plastic wrap, and chill 30 minutes.

2 Grease the outer sides and base of six ⅔-cup dariole molds or ovenproof cups and put them upside down on a baking sheet. Roll out the dough on a lightly floured surface until about ¼ inch thick. Cut out 6 circles, each about 4¼ inches wide, and drape each one over the top of a dariole mold. Gently mold the dough over the molds to make "cups" and chill 30 minutes.

3 Preheat the oven to 400°F, then bake the pastry cups 30 minutes or until light golden and crisp, then remove them from the molds. Return the cups, right-side up, to the oven still on the baking sheet and bake 10 minutes longer. Transfer to a wire rack to cool.

4 While the pastry cups are baking, roast the Jerusalem artichoke. Lightly toss the artichoke slices in the olive oil and spread them out on a baking sheet. Bake 30 minutes, turning once, until light golden and crisp in places.

5 Meanwhile, prepare the filling. Cook the celery root in boiling salted water 10 minutes or until tender. Drain well, then return them to the pan. Add the butter and milk and warm over low heat, then transfer to a blender and puree until smooth and creamy. Season with salt and pepper and stir in the parsley.

6 Divide the celeriac puree into the pastry cups and top with the dolcelatte. Stand 1 slice of the roasted Jerusalem artichoke (you might have a few slices left over) upright in the middle of each tart and serve warm with roasted potatoes.

# SWEET POTATO AND GOAT CHEESE GALETTES

Orange-fleshed sweet potatoes take on an almost caramel sweetness when baked, which goes well with the North African spices and crisp puff pastry crust of these galettes.

**SERVES 4**

1 pound 8 ounces sweet potatoes
2 tablespoons olive oil, plus extra for greasing
10 ounces puff pastry dough
all-purpose flour, for rolling the dough
1 egg, lightly beaten
¼ cup crème fraîche or sour cream
1 red chili, seeded and finely sliced
2 teaspoons za'atar (see page 156) or cumin seeds
3 ounces goat cheese, cut into chunks
1 small garlic clove, crushed
finely grated zest of 1 small lemon
2 tablespoons chopped parsley leaves
salt and freshly ground black pepper

1 Preheat the oven to 400°F. Bake the sweet potatoes 40 to 45 minutes until tender. Set aside until cool enough to handle, then peel and cut into ¼-inch slices.

2 While the sweet potatoes are baking, grease a baking sheet with olive oil and set aside. Roll out the dough on a lightly floured surface and cut it into 4 rectangles, each about 6 x 3½ inches. Put them on the baking sheet and brush with the egg, then, using a sharp knife, lightly score a border around each dough rectangle, about ½ inch from the edges.

3 Spread 1 tablespoon of the crème fraîche over each dough rectangle, keeping it within the border. Arrange the slices of sweet potato, slightly overlapping, on top of the crème fraîche and sprinkle with the chili and za'atar. Top with the goat cheese and season with salt and pepper.

4 Bake the galettes 25 minutes or until the pastry is golden. Take a peek under the galettes to make sure the bottom is baked. Meanwhile, mix together the olive oil, garlic, lemon zest, and parsley in a small bowl.

5 Drizzle the dressing over the galettes and serve.

# OVEN-ROASTED RATATOUILLE IN TORTILLA BASKETS

Roasting concentrates the natural sugars in vegetables, enriching and enhancing their flavor and giving them a soft, almost caramelized texture.

**SERVES 4**

1 eggplant, sliced and then quartered

2 zucchini, thickly sliced

1 red bell pepper, seeded and cut into 1-inch pieces

1 yellow bell pepper, seeded and cut into 1-inch pieces

1 large fennel bulb, thickly sliced

2 onions, each cut into 6 wedges

3 large garlic cloves, thickly sliced

8 tomatoes, halved

7 tablespoons olive oil

3 rosemary sprigs

4 oregano sprigs

4 thyme sprigs

4 small soft flour tortillas

4 large eggs, at room temperature

basil leaves, to decorate

salt and freshly ground black pepper

crème fraîche, to serve (optional)

1 Preheat the oven to 425°F. Put the eggplant, zucchini, red and yellow peppers, fennel, onions, garlic, and tomatoes in a large bowl. Drizzle with the olive oil and toss well. Divide the vegetables onto two large baking trays and tuck in the rosemary, oregano, and thyme. Roast 20 minutes, then remove the herbs.

2 Turn the vegetables and return the trays to the oven, swapping them over. Roast 15 minutes longer, or until the vegetables are tender and caramelized in places. Season with salt and pepper, sprinkle with some basil leaves, and set aside, covered, while you make the tortilla baskets.

3 Reduce the oven to 350°F and lightly grease four 1¼-cup ovenproof bowls or mugs. Drape a tortilla over each bowl, gently pressing them down to form a cup shape. Put the bowls upside down on baking sheets and bake 10 minutes or until the tortillas are golden and crisp, then let cool slightly.

4 Meanwhile, bring a small saucepan of water to a boil and carefully add the eggs. Return to a boil, then reduce the heat to medium and cook 5 minutes. Remove the eggs from the pan and rinse under cold running water 1 minute to stop them from cooking any farther. Set aside and peel when cool enough to handle.

5 To serve, divide the ratatouille into the tortilla baskets. Cut the hard-boiled eggs in half lengthwise and put 2 halves on top of each portion of ratatouille. Serve topped with crème fraîche, if desired.

# POTATO, CELERY ROOT, AND PORCINI MUSHROOM GRATIN

**SERVES 4**

¾ ounce dried porcini mushrooms

2 tablespoons butter

1 tablespoon olive oil

3 garlic cloves, thinly sliced

1¼ cups heavy cream

¼ cup milk

2 cups peeled and sliced (¼-inch thick) celery root

3½ unpeeled potatoes cut into ¼-inch slices

salt and freshly ground black pepper

1 Put the porcini mushrooms in a small bowl, cover with ½ cup boiled water and let soak 20 minutes. Strain the soaking liquid into a clean bowl and set aside, and then coarsely chop the mushrooms.

2 Heat the butter and olive oil in a large skillet and fry the garlic 1 minute, stirring. Add the porcini and cook 1 minute longer, stirring. Add the mushroom soaking liquid to the pan. Add the cream and milk, then season well with salt and pepper. Add the celery root and potatoes and gently turn to coat them in the creamy mixture. Bring to a boil, then reduce the heat to low and simmer, covered, 20 minutes or until the potatoes and celery root are tender but not too soft.

3 Meanwhile, preheat the oven to 425°F. Transfer the potato and celeriac mixture to a 10½- x 8-inch baking dish and bake 35 minutes or until the top is golden and the vegetables are tender. Serve hot.

# BAKED FONTINA, CARAWAY, AND BUCKWHEAT PASTA

**SERVES 4**

2 potatoes, peeled and cubed

9 ounces buckwheat penne

3½ cups shredded savoy cabbage

3 tablespoons olive oil, plus extra for greasing

1 large onion, finely chopped

2 garlic cloves, finely chopped

2½ cups sliced cremini mushrooms

2 teaspoons caraway seeds

1 teaspoon cumin seeds

1 cup less 2 tablespoons hot vegetable stock

heaped 1 cup cubed Fontina cheese,

¼ cup coarsely chopped walnuts

salt and freshly ground black pepper

1 Preheat the oven to 400°F and grease a large, deep baking dish with oil. Cook the potatoes in salted boiling water 8 minutes, or until just tender, then drain and set aside.

2 Meanwhile, cook the pasta in boiling salted water until it is just cooked and remains al dente (about 2 minutes less than stated on the package directions). Add the savoy cabbage in the last minute of cooking, then drain and rinse under cold running water to stop the cooking process.

3 Heat the olive oil in a large, nonstick saucepan over medium-low heat. Fry the onions 8 minutes, stirring occasionally, until golden and soft. Add the garlic, mushrooms, and caraway and cumin seeds and cook 4 minutes longer, or until tender.

4 Remove the pan from the heat and add the potatoes, pasta, cabbage, and stock. Stir until combined, then season with salt and pepper. Transfer to the baking dish and top with the Fontina and walnuts. Bake 20 minutes or until the cheese is bubbling and golden, then serve.

# PARMESAN ROULADE WITH KABOCHA SQUASH

The beauty of a roulade is that is can be prepared in advance—and despite its impressive appearance, it's relatively easy to make. Serve with arugula and spinach salad, if desired. If you can't find kabocha, you can also use acorn or butternut squash.

**SERVES 6**

¼ cup butter
scant ⅓ cup all-purpose flour
1¼ cups milk
heaped ½ cup grated sharp cheddar
  cheese
½ cup finely-grated Parmesan
  cheese
4 large eggs, separated
salt and freshly ground black pepper

**FILLING**

2⅓ cups peeled, seeded, and diced
  kabocha squash
3 garlic cloves
2 tablespoons cream cheese
1 heaped teaspoon Dijon mustard
1 handful of cilantro leaves, chopped
1 handful of flat-leaf parsley leaves,
  chopped

1 Preheat the oven to 375°F and line a 12- x 9-inch baking tray with baking parchment paper. Melt the butter in a large nonstick saucepan. Add the flour and cook 1 minute, stirring continuously. Gradually stir in the milk. Bring to a boil, stirring, until the sauce is thick and smooth. Remove the pan from the heat and stir in the cheddar and three-quarters of the Parmesan until they melt. Beat in the egg yolks and season with salt and pepper.

2 In a large, clean bowl, beat the egg whites until they form stiff peaks. Fold a spoonful of the egg whites into the cheese sauce, then fold in the rest until incorporated, taking care not to lose too much volume. Pour the batter into the baking tray and gently spread out into an even layer. Bake 15 minutes or until risen and golden.

3 Meanwhile, steam the squash 5 minutes, then add the garlic and continue steaming 5 minutes longer, or until tender. Puree the squash, garlic, cream cheese, and mustard in a blender, then set aside to cool.

4 Sprinkle the remaining Parmesan over a sheet of baking parchment paper about the same size as the baking tray. Remove the roulade from the oven, turn it out onto the paper and peel off the paper lining it was baked on. Trim and discard the crisp outer edges of the roulade.

5 Spread the squash mixture over the roulade. Sprinkle the cilantro and parsley leaves lengthwise down the middle and season with salt and pepper. Using the baking parchment paper to help guide you, roll up the roulade from a short end as tightly as possible to form a log. Discard the paper, cut the roulade into slices, and serve.

# ROSEMARY AND SEA SALT CRUSHED POTATOES

These crisp, golden new potatoes (pictured, page 212) make an excellent alternative to traditional roast spuds. Make sure the potatoes are about the same size so they cook evenly.

**SERVES 6**

2 pounds 4 ounces new potatoes, scrubbed, whole and unpeeled
2 tablespoons olive oil
3 tablespoons butter, cut into small pieces
2 long rosemary sprigs
salt flakes

1 Preheat the oven to 425°F. Boil the potatoes 15 minutes or until partially cooked, then drain well.
2 Put the olive oil in a large roasting pan and heat in the oven 3 minutes. Using the back of a fork, crush the top of each potato —they should keep their shape but have a "cracked" top half. Arrange the potatoes in the pan in a single layer, spaced slightly apart.
3 Put a small piece of the butter on top of each potato and sprinkle with a few flakes of salt. Roast the potatoes 20 minutes.
4 Pull the leaves off the rosemary in small sprigs and insert 2 or 3 into the top of each potato. Roast 15 to 20 minutes until crisp and golden, then serve.

# PARMESAN-CRUSTED PARSNIPS

Finely grated Parmesan cheese gives these roasted parsnips a delightful golden crust.

**SERVES 4**

3 parsnips, peeled and halved or quartered, if large
3 tablespoons finely grated Parmesan cheese
scant 1/3 cup all-purpose flour
2 tablespoons olive oil
4 teaspoons butter
salt and freshly ground black pepper

1 Preheat the oven to 375°F. Meanwhile, boil the parsnips 3 minutes or until slightly tender.
2 Meanwhile, mix together the Parmesan and flour in a large bowl and season with salt and pepper.
3 Drain the parsnips and while still hot and steamy and toss them, a few at a time, in the Parmesan mixture until coated.
4 Put half of the olive oil in a large roasting tray and heat it in the oven 2 minutes. Meanwhile, heat the butter and remaining oil in a small saucepan until melted. Arrange the parsnips in the tray in a single layer and brush the tops with the butter and oil mixture. Roast 40 minutes, turning once, until golden and crisp all over, then serve.

## BAKED VEGETABLES IN A BAG

The baking parchment paper packages help to retain the juices from the vegetables while they cook, preventing them from drying out and producing a fresh and simple sauce. You can also top the vegetables with a spoonful of pesto and a few shavings of Parmesan just before serving, if you like.

**SERVES 4**

2 tablespoons olive oil
2 tablespoons verjuice or white wine vinegar
2 red onions, peeled and each cut into 6 wedges with the stem intact
8 large garlic cloves
1 fennel bulb, cut into wedges
2 zucchini, halved and cut into batons
2 handfuls of cherry tomatoes
1 small handful of basil leaves
salt and freshly ground black pepper

1 Preheat the oven 375°F. Mix together the olive oil and verjuice in a large bowl. Add the onions, garlic, fennel, zucchini, and tomatoes and turn them until coated in the mixture.

2 Take 2 large sheets of baking parchment paper and divide the vegetables between them, placing them in the middle. Season the vegetables with salt and pepper and top with a few basil leaves. Gather up the paper and secure to make 2 packages, either by securing with string or folding the edges over to seal. Put the packages in baking trays and roast 45 minutes or until the vegetables are tender.

3 Carefully open the packages and remove the cooked basil leaves. Top with basil leaves and serve.

## ROASTED GARLIC WITH CHAR-BROILED TOAST

Roasted garlic takes on a subtle flavor and loses its harsh pungency. It also takes on a wonderful creamy texture, making it almost spreadable. It's delicious spread on hot toast.

**SERVES 4**

2 garlic bulbs
1 tablespoon olive oil, plus extra for drizzling
4 thick slices of rustic-style bread
salt and freshly ground black pepper

1 Preheat the oven to 350°F. Slice the top of each bulb of garlic so the cloves are just exposed. Put each bulb on a piece of foil large enough to enclose it. Drizzle with the olive oil and pull up the foil to loosely enclose.

2 Put the packages in a baking tray and roast 30 to 40 minutes, or until the cloves are soft and tender. When cool enough to handle, squeeze the softened cloves out of the skins and into a small bowl.

3 Heat a griddle pan over medium heat and toast both sides of the bread until blackened in places. Spread the garlic over each slice, season with salt and pepper, and drizzle with a little more oil, then serve.

# ROASTED BALSAMIC PEARS

Roasted until tender and slightly caramelized, the pears make a great accompaniment to the Mushroom and Cashew Pies (see page 204).

**SERVES 4**
4 pears
1 tablespoon lemon juice
2 tablespoons balsamic vinegar
1 tablespoon olive oil
salt and freshly ground black pepper

1 Preheat the oven to 400°F. Peel the pears and cut them in half lengthwise, then brush with the lemon juice to prevent them from discoloring.
2 Mix together the balsamic vinegar and olive oil and season with salt and pepper. Brush the pears with the balsamic mixture, put them on a baking tray and 30 to 35 minutes until tender and golden, then serve.

# EGGPLANT CAVIAR

This version of the Middle Eastern classic eggplant dish, baba ganoush, is baked in the oven until meltingly soft.

**SERVES 4**
2 eggplants
2 garlic cloves, crushed
juice of 1 large lemon
2 tablespoons light tahini
1 teaspoon ground cumin
¼ cup plain yogurt
salt and freshly ground black pepper

1 Preheat the oven to 425°F. Prick the eggplants all over and put them on a baking try. Roast 45 to 50 minutes until the inside is soft.
2 Scoop out the eggplant flesh, discarding the skin, and chop the flesh finely. Transfer the chopped eggplant to a bowl and stir in the garlic, lemon juice, tahini, cumin, and yogurt until smooth and creamy. Season with salt and pepper to taste and serve.

# ROASTED PLUM VERRINES WITH TOFFEE PECANS

Verrines are individual layered glassfuls of deliciousness—in this case a sweetened rosewater cream, slow-roasted spiced plums, amaretti cookies, and toffee-coated pecans. The desserts can be made a few hours in advance and chilled, but bring them back to room temperature before serving.

**SERVES 4**

1 cup plus 2 tablespoons heavy
   cream
2 tablespoons confectioners' sugar
1 teaspoon rosewater
8 amaretti cookies, broken

SLOW-ROASTED PLUMS
⅔ cup freshly squeezed orange juice
1 teaspoon lemon juice
½ teaspoon cinnamon
2 cloves
1 star anise
2 tablespoons granulated sugar
7 ounces plums, halved and pitted

TOFFEE PECANS
2 tablespoons butter
3 tablespoons granulated sugar
1½ cup pecan halves

1 To make the plums, mix together the orange and lemon juice, cinnamon, cloves, star anise, and sugar in a large bowl. Add the plums and turn until soaked. Remove the plums from the bowl reserving the orange juice mixture, and arrange the plums, cut-side down, on a baking sheet. Put the plums in a cold oven, turn it on and set the temperature to 315°F. Roast 1 hour, or until slightly shriveled and softened.

2 About 10 minutes before the plums are ready, put the orange juice mixture in a saucepan and bring to a boil. Reduce the heat to low and simmer 5 to 8 minutes until thick and syrupy. Remove the pan from the heat, add the roasted plums, and let cool. Remove and discard the whole spices.

3 Meanwhile, make the toffee pecans. Line a baking sheet with baking parchment paper. Melt the butter in a small, nonstick skillet and add the sugar. Stir over medium-low heat 5 minutes or until the sugar melts and turns golden. Remove the pan from the heat and add the pecans, stirring until coated in the syrup, then spoon onto the baking sheet, spreading them apart. Let cool.

4 Whip the cream until it forms soft peaks, then beat in the confectioners' sugar and rosewater. Roughly chop three-quarters of the pecans and mix with the broken amaretti cookies.

5 In four glasses, arrange layers of the amaretti and pecan mixture, rosewater cream, and plums with a little bit of their syrup. Top each portion with more cream and a few of the reserved pecans and serve.

# MAPLE FIGS WITH CARDAMOM SHORTBREAD

You want delicious just-ripe figs for this recipe—not too soft or they will lose their shape during baking.

**SERVES 4 TO 6**

12 figs
5 tablespoons maple syrup
½ teaspoon cinnamon
3 tablespoons freshly squeezed orange juice
zest of 1 orange
4 teaspoons butter
⅔ cup Greek yogurt, to serve

CARDAMOM SHORTBREAD

7 tablespoons butter, softened, plus extra for greasing
½ cup confectioners' sugar, plus extra for dusting
a pinch of salt
scant ⅔ cup all-purpose flour, sifted, plus extra for rolling the dough
heaped ¼ cup rice flour or cornstarch, sifted
seeds from 5 cardamom pods, crushed
granulated sugar, for dusting

1 First, make the cardamom shortbread. Preheat the oven to 315°F and lightly grease an 8- x 4½-inch baking pan (or section of a baking tray, because the shortbread keeps its shape during baking). Using an electric mixer, cream the butter and confectioners' sugar together 6 to 8 minutes until light and fluffy, then add the salt, both flours, and cardamom seeds and beat until incorporated. Using your hands, press the mixture together to form a smooth ball of dough, then wrap in plastic wrap, and chill 30 minutes.

2 Roll out the dough on a lightly floured surface to about ⅝ inch thick. It will be very crumbly but don't worry. Press it into the pan and bake 25 to 30 minutes until pale golden and crisp. Dust the shortbread with granulated sugar and cut into 8 fingers, each 4½ inches long, and cool in the pan while you prepare the figs.

3 Increase the oven temperature to 375°F. Using a small, sharp knife, cut a cross in the top of each fig, cutting halfway down to the bottom. Stand the figs upright in a roasting pan, opening them out slightly, and set aside.

4 Put the maple syrup, cinnamon, orange juice and zest, and butter in a saucepan and bring to a boil, then reduce the heat to low. Cook, stirring continuously, 3 to 5 minutes, until syrupy and thick. Spoon the sauce over the figs and bake 10 to 15 minutes until soft. Serve the figs warm or at room temperature with any juices in the pan and with the shortbread fingers and yogurt.

# VEGAN CHOCOLATE CAKE WITH MAPLE DRIZZLE

This cake is amazing—it's a wonder that it works and it does so with great results! A breeze to make, you simply just mix everything together and it holds together and rises perfectly, even though there are not any eggs or butter.

**SERVES 12**

5 tablespoons sunflower oil, plus
   extra for greasing
1²/₃ cups all-purpose flour
1 cup plus 2 tablespoons granulated
   sugar
1 teaspoon baking soda
¹/₂ teaspoon salt
3 tablespoons unsweetened cocoa
   powder
1 teaspoon vanilla extract
1 tablespoon distilled vinegar or
   white vinegar

**MAPLE DRIZZLE**

6 tablespoons vegan cream cheese
¹/₃ cup confectioners' sugar
1 teaspoon vanilla extract
1 tablespoon maple syrup

1 Preheat the oven to 350°F and lightly grease an 8¹/₂- x 4¹/₂-inch bread pan with sunflower oil.

2 In a large bowl, sift together the flour, sugar, baking soda, salt, and cocoa powder, mixing until combined. In a separate bowl, mix together the oil, vanilla extract, vinegar, and 1 cup plus 2 tablespoons water. Add the wet mixture to the dry ingredients and stir until smooth.

3 Pour the batter into the pan and bake 45 to 50 minutes until risen —a skewer inserted in the middle of the cake should come out clean. Let cool for 5 minutes before turning out of the pan onto a wire rack to cool completely.

4 To make the maple drizzle, beat together the cream cheese, confectioners' sugar, vanilla extract, and maple syrup until smooth. Chill 30 minutes to thicken slightly. Cut the cake into slices, drizzle each slice with a spoonful of the maple drizzle, and serve.

# PEAR, BANANA, AND CHOCOLATE WONTONS

**SERVES 4**

sunflower oil, for greasing

16 wonton wrappers

½ small just-ripe pear (not too soft), peeled, halved, and thinly sliced

2 ounces dark chocolate, broken or chopped into 8 equal pieces

1 small banana, sliced

2 tablespoons butter, melted

confectioners' sugar, for dusting

**1** Preheat the oven to 375°F and lightly grease two baking sheets with sunflower oil. Put 1 wonton wrapper on a work surface and put 1 slice of the pear and 1 chunk of the chocolate in the middle. Brush the edges of the wrapper with water and cover with a second wrapper. Press the edges together to seal, then put the wonton package on the baking sheet. Repeat to make 3 more pear and chocolate wonton packages, then make 4 more packages using the banana and the remaining chocolate (you will have some fruit leftover).

**2** Brush the packages with the melted butter and bake 10 minutes until golden and crisp.

**3** Dust the wonton packages with a little confectioners' sugar and serve, allowing one banana and one pear wonton per person.


# PUMPKIN CHEESECAKE

**SERVES 8 TO 10**

8 ounces pumpkin or kabocha squash, seeded and cut into wedges

1¼ cups cream cheese

1 cup plus 2 tablespoons ricotta cheese

heaped 1 cup granulated sugar

2 teaspoons vanilla extract

3 large eggs

whole nutmeg, for grating

finely sliced zest of 1 unwaxed lemon, to decorate

light cream, to serve

CRUST

4 ounces graham crackers

scant ½ cup very finely ground blanched almonds

¼ cup butter, melted, plus extra for greasing

**1** Preheat the oven to 400°F. Grease the sides of a deep 8-inch springform cake pan with melted butter and line the bottom with baking parchment paper. Stand the pumpkin wedges on a baking tray and roast 25 to 30 minutes until tender, then remove from the oven and reduce the oven temperature to 300°F.

**2** Meanwhile, make the crust. Put the crackers in a food processor and pulse until fine, then transfer to a bowl and mix in the almonds and butter until combined. Press the mixture in an even layer into the bottom of the pan and chill until required.

**3** Remove and discard the skin from the pumpkin and puree the flesh in a food processor or blender for a few seconds until smooth. Press the puree through a strainer to remove any fibers.

**4** Put the cream cheese and ricotta in the food processor and blend until smooth, then add the pumpkin puree, sugar, vanilla extract, and eggs and process again until combined. Pour the batter onto the crust and bake 1 hour 10 minutes or until set but still a little wobbly. Remove the pan from the oven and let the cheesecake cool in the pan.

**5** Grate a generous amount of nutmeg over the cheesecake, sprinkle with the lemon zest, and serve with light cream.

# CHOCOLATE TRUFFLE TORTE WITH AMARETTO CREAM

This rich and indulgent cake is slightly gooey in the middle, its intense chocolate truffle topping complemented by the crisp amaretti and roasted hazelnut crust. The amaretto-infused cream makes a decadent accompaniment, while fresh strawberries or raspberries are perfect partners, too.

**SERVES 10 TO 12**

6 ounces dark chocolate, broken into pieces
¾ cup plus 2 tablespoons granulated sugar
⅔ cup unsalted butter
4 extra-large eggs, separated
1 teaspoon vanilla extract
scant 1 cup very finely ground blanched almonds
unsweetened cocoa powder, for dusting

**HAZELNUT AND AMARETTI CRUST**

¼ cup butter, plus extra for greasing
all-purpose flour, for dusting
¼ cup whole skinned hazelnuts
6 ounces amaretti cookies

**AMARETTO CREAM**

1¼ cups heavy cream
1 tablespoon amaretto liqueur, or to taste
1 tablespoon confectioners' sugar, or to taste

**1** First, make the crust. Preheat the oven to 350°F. Lightly grease and flour the sides of an 8-inch springform cake pan and line the bottom with baking parchment paper. Put the hazelnuts on a baking tray and toast 6 to 7 minutes until lightly colored. Remove from the oven and let cool.

**2** Put the hazelnuts and amaretti cookies in a food processor and pulse until finely ground. Melt the butter in a medium saucepan over medium-low heat. Remove the pan from the heat and stir in the cookies and nuts until combined. Press the cookie mixture into the bottom of the cake pan to make a firm, even layer. Set aside while you make the truffle filling.

**3** Put the chocolate in a heatproof bowl and rest it over a pan of gently simmering water, making sure the bottom of the bowl does not touch the water. Heat 4 to 5 minutes, stirring occasionally, until the chocolate melts, then set aside to cool slightly.

**4** Cream the granulated sugar and butter in a mixing bowl until light and fluffy. Beat in the egg yolks, one at a time, then beat in the vanilla extract and melted chocolate. When thoroughly blended, mix in the ground almonds.

**5** In a clean bowl, beat the egg whites until they form stiff peaks, then fold them into the cake batter in three batches. Pour the batter over the crust. Bake 40 to 45 minutes until baked on the outside but still slightly runny in the middle. Don't worry if it cracks a little. Remove the cake from the oven and let cool in the pan.

**6** To make the amaretto cream, whip the cream in a clean bowl until it starts to thicken, then add the liqueur and confectioners' sugar. Continue whipping until soft peaks form. Taste and add more liqueur or sugar, if desired.

**7** Dust the cake with a layer of cocoa powder and serve with a large spoonful of the amaretto cream.

# CARAMELIZED LEMON AND ALMOND TART

Tangy with an intense lemon flavor, this tart has a golden caramelized top and a spelt dough. Spelt is an ancient form of wheat and produces a slightly nutty flavored crust, but you can also use all-purpose flour.

**SERVES 8**
2 eggs
¼ cup granulated sugar
finely grated zest and juice
    of 4 unwaxed lemons
1 teaspoon vanilla extract
¼ cup very finely ground blanched
    almonds
½ cup light cream
3 tablespoons confectioners' sugar

**PASTRY DOUGH**
1¾ cups spelt flour, plus extra for
    rolling the dough
heaped ½ cup confectioners' sugar
a pinch of salt
½ cup chilled butter, plus extra for
    greasing
1 large egg, lightly beaten

1  First make the pastry dough. Sift the flour, confectioners' sugar, and salt into a mixing bowl. Rub in the butter with your fingertips until the mixture resembles fine bread crumbs, then add the egg and mix to combine. Press the dough together to make a smooth ball, then flatten into a ball, wrap in plastic wrap, and chill 20 minutes.

2  Lightly grease a 9-inch loose-bottomed tart pan with butter. Roll out the dough on a lightly floured surface and then press it gently into the pan. Prick the dough all over with a fork and chill 15 minutes.

3  Meanwhile, preheat the oven to 350°F. Line the tart shell with baking parchment paper and fill with baking beans, then bake 10 minutes. Remove the baking beans and paper and bake 10 minutes longer, until light golden.

4  Meanwhile, make the filling. Put the eggs and granulated sugar in a large bowl and beat with an electric mixer 5 to 7 minutes until the mixture is pale and thick enough to leave a trail when the beaters are lifted. Stir in the lemon zest and juice, vanilla extract, ground almonds, and cream. Pour the filling into the tart shell and bake 25 minutes or until set.

5  Heat the broiler to high. Sift the confectioners' sugar evenly over the tart and broil 1 to 2 minutes until the sugar melts and caramelizes —watch carefully to make sure it doesn't burn. Let the tart cool slightly. Serve warm or at room temperature.

# RHUBARB AND CUSTARD TARTLETS

These pretty tartlets are made with sour cream pastry dough, which has a light and flaky texture and holds together well when rolled out. The rhubarb is baked until soft and slightly caramelized.

**MAKES 10**

1 cup plus 2 tablespoons milk

5 tablespoons light cream

1 extra-large egg

1 egg yolk

heaped ¼ cup granulated sugar

1 teaspoon vanilla extract

**SOUR CREAM PASTRY DOUGH**

7 tablespoons cold butter, diced, plus extra for greasing

1 cup less 1½ tablespoons all-purpose flour, sifted, plus extra for rolling the dough

¼ cup sour cream

**RHUBARB**

2 tablespoons butter

5 tablespoons maple syrup

2⅓ cups rhubarb cut into 1-inch pieces

1 To make the sour cream pastry dough, put the butter and flour into a food processor and pulse until they resemble fine bread crumbs. Add the sour cream and continue pulsing until the dough starts to come together. Remove the dough from the food processor, shape into a ball, wrap in plastic wrap, and chill 30 minutes.

2 Meanwhile, preheat the oven to 350°F and grease 10 holes of a deep muffin pan with butter. Roll out the dough on a lightly floured surface to about ⅛ inch thick. Cut out 10 circles, slightly larger than the muffin cups and press them gently into the muffin pan. Chill for 30 minutes.

3 Gently heat the milk and cream in a small saucepan until almost boiling. In a bowl, beat together the egg, egg yolk, sugar, and vanilla extract until pale, then gradually beat in the milk mixture. Set aside and let cool.

4 Pour the egg mixture evenly into the dough cups and bake 30 to 35 minutes until the pastry is golden and the custard is just set.

5 Meanwhile, cook the rhubarb. Melt the butter in a nonstick pan over medium-low heat, add the maple syrup, and then the rhubarb. Turn the rhubarb in the hot syrup mixture 2 minutes. Arrange the rhubarb pieces in an even layer on a nonstick parchment baking sheet and spoon a little of the syrup mixture over them. Bake 25 minutes, turning once and spooning a little more of the syrup over rhubarb pieces, until the are tender and slightly caramelized.

6 Remove the tartlets and rhubarb from the oven. Let the tartlets cool in the muffin pan, then transfer to a wire rack. Let the rhubarb cool. Top the tartlets with some of the rhubarb and serve.

# MERINGUE WITH TOASTED HAZELNUTS AND BUTTERSCOTCH SAUCE

This meringue is cooked at a higher temperature than usual, so the addition of cornstarch and vinegar in the batter gives it a delicious combination of gooey middle and crisp outer shell. The result is a perfect marriage of marshmallow-centred meringue, toasted hazelnuts, vanilla cream, rich butterscotch sauce, and fresh raspberries.

**SERVES 6 TO 8**

½ cup hazelnuts
5 extra-large egg whites
1½ cups granulated sugar
1 teaspoon cornstarch
1 teaspoon white wine vinegar
1¾ cups heavy cream
1 teaspoon vanilla extract
1½ cups fresh raspberries

**BUTTERSCOTCH SAUCE**

1 cup golden syrup or ⅔ cup light corn syrup
3 tablespoons granulated sugar
3 tablespoons light brown sugar
¼ cup butter
½ cup heavy cream

1 Preheat the oven to 350°F. Roast the hazelnuts in a baking tray 6 to 8 minutes until toasted, taking care as they can easily burn. Transfer the nuts into a clean dish towel, gather up the edges to make a bundle and rub the nuts to remove the skins. Let cool, then coarsely chop and set aside.

2 Beat the egg whites in a clean bowl until they form stiff peaks. Add the granulated sugar a little bit at a time, beating after each addition. Continue bating 3 to 4 minutes until the meringue is stiff and glossy, then beat in the vinegar and cornstarch.

3 Line a large baking sheet with baking parchment paper. Heap the meringue into a rough 8-inch circle on the baking sheet and make a slight well in the middle. Bake in the middle of the oven 40 to 45 minutes until light golden and crisp on the outside but still soft in the middle. Turn off the oven, open the door. and leave the meringue inside to cool completely.

4 Meanwhile, make the butterscotch sauce. Put the syrup, granulated sugar, brown sugar, and butter in a saucepan and bring to a boil, then reduce the heat to low and cook, stirring occasionally, 5 minutes until thicker. Remove the pan from the heat and stir in the cream. Let cool and thicken more.

5 Transfer the meringue to a serving plate. Just before serving, whip the cream and vanilla extract together until soft peaks form, then heap it on top of the meringue. Sprinkle with the toasted hazelnuts and drizzle with the butterscotch sauce (you will have some left over). Sprinkle the raspberries over the top and serve.

# PINEAPPLE AND COCONUT SOUFFLÉS

Soufflés have a reputation for being tricky to make but this one couldn't be more well-behaved, producing a light and fluffy dessert with a touch of the Caribbean.

**SERVES 4**

3 tablespoons shredded coconut
butter, for greasing
3 extra-large eggs, separated
scant ⅓ cup granulated sugar
7 ounces canned pineapple chunks
  in natural juice, drained and finely
  chopped
confectioners' sugar, for dusting

1 Preheat the oven to 375°F and lightly butter four ⅔-cup ramekins with butter. Put half of the coconut on a baking sheet and toast 2 minutes or until golden, then set aside.

2 Beat together the egg yolks and half of the sugar 5 to 7 minutes until light and fluffy. Stir in the pineapple and the untoasted coconut and set aside.

3 Beat the egg whites in a clean bowl until stiff peaks form, then add the remaining sugar in two batches, continuing to beat until thick and glossy. Gradually and gently fold the mixture into the pineapple mixture, taking care not to lose too much volume.

4 Spoon the soufflé mixture into the ramekins, filling them to the brim, and smooth the tops with a metal spatula. Bake 10 minutes or until risen and golden. Sift a little confectioners' sugar over the top, sprinkle with the toasted coconut and serve immediately.

# APPLE, HONEY, AND ROSEMARY CLAFOUTIS

This classic French dessert is given a twist with the addition of honey and a hint of fresh rosemary.

**SERVES 6**

⅔ cup milk
½ cup heavy cream
2-inch rosemary sprig
3 tablespoons honey
butter, for greasing
3 large eggs
a pinch of salt
⅓ cup plus 1 tablespoon granulated
  sugar
scant ⅓ cup all-purpose flour
2 apples, peeled, cored, halved, and
  thinly sliced
confectioners' sugar, for dusting

1 Put the milk, cream, rosemary, and honey in a saucepan and stir well to dissolve the honey. Bring to a boil, then remove from the heat and let infuse 25 minutes. Remove and discard the rosemary.

2 Preheat the oven to 350°F and lightly grease a 10½ - x 8-inch baking dish with butter. In a large bowl, beat the eggs, salt, and sugar 6 to 8 minutes until pale, fluffy, and more than doubled in volume. Fold in the flour and then the milk mixture. Pour the batter into the baking dish and arrange the apple slices over the top —they will sink slightly into the batter.

3 Bake 35 minutes or until risen and golden. Sift confectioners' sugar over the top and serve warm.

# INDEX